# LEARNING AND MEMORY

## AN INTRODUCTION

# LEARNING AND MEMORY

## AN INTRODUCTION

**JAMES L. McGAUGH**
UNIVERSITY OF CALIFORNIA, IRVINE

**ALBION PUBLISHING COMPANY**
SAN FRANCISCO

ALBION PUBLISHING COMPANY
1736 STOCKTON STREET
SAN FRANCISCO, CALIFORNIA 94133

Library of Congress Catalog Card Number 72-84850
ISBN 0 87843 608 1
Printed in the United States of America

Parts of this work from Psychology by Harlow, McGaugh, and
Thompson, copyright © 1971 by Albion Publishing Company,
reprinted by permission.

TO BECKY

# PREFACE

One of the most obvious facts of experience is that we are profoundly influenced by our experiences. Our ability to learn and remember allows us to alter our behavior to fit the requirements of an ever-changing environment and provides a basis for the complex processes of thought, language, and intelligence.

This book is a brief introduction to the phenomena of learning and memory. We know a great deal about the conditions under which learning occurs. But, as yet, we know little about the bases of learning. The nature of the "machinery" underlying learning, memory, and complex intellectual processes is perhaps the most intriguing as well as important scientific problem. And, of course, it is of immense practical importance that we understand these phenomena since our behavior depends so fundamentally upon the cumulative and lasting effects of our experiences.

Many individuals have influenced the development of this book and I gratefully acknowledge these influences. I thank my colleague Richard F. Thompson for his contribution to Chapter 3 (Thought and Language). Karen Dodd was responsible for preparing the several drafts of the chapters and for attending to all of the details involved in preparing the manuscript for publication. I thank her for her expert assistance. I also thank those who have permitted me to quote or reproduce material from their works. Finally, I thank my teachers and students and colleagues for their influences on my learning about learning.

JAMES L. McGAUGH

# CONTENTS

# CHAPTER ONE

## LEARNING AND BEHAVIORAL ADAPTATION

As we know from our everyday observations, our behavior is profoundly influenced by our experiences. We have learned to talk, to read, to write, to plan, to hope, and to love. We have also learned to deceive, to fear, and perhaps to hate. Learning in its broadest sense makes human socialization possible. Society is based on the training provided by subtle as well as explicit experiences, such as formal education. Because of our enormous capacity for learning, human behavior can be and is extremely varied. For example, as humans we inherit molecules that program the neurobiological processes which make it possible for us to acquire and use language. However, the language each of us learns is the language spoken by those around us. So it is with all our skills, habits, aspirations, beliefs, and prejudices. For centuries scholars have wondered what human beings would be like if they were reared in isolation from other human beings. One speculation was that children reared in cultural isolation might speak some basic or "natural" human language. In all likelihood, however, they would acquire no language at all. They would in fact lack most of the characteristics that we regard as distinctively "human." We learn to be human beings.

# LEARNING

Since it is learning that enables us to adapt to the complex requirements of our environments, it might be well to begin with a biological perspective of learning. The basis of evolution is adaptation. The survival of any species depends on its ability to adapt to the requirements of its own particular environment. There are, of course, many ways in which adaptation takes place. Through the slow process of genetic mutation and selection a species can acquire the necessary form and physiological machinery for almost any environmental condition. For example, many species, such as the polar bear, have evolved a coloration that serves as camouflage in their natural surroundings. The physiology of such arctic animals is also quite different from that of desert animals. Adaptation is particularly apparent in behavior. Lower animals can, without specific training, perform many complicated tasks, such as nest building, migrating, communicating, and mating. The development of such genetically influenced responses, commonly referred to as *instincts*, provides for rather complex behavioral adaptation to special environments. However, organisms sometimes become so specialized in form or function that they are unable to survive. In a complex environment the evolution of unique morphological, physiological, or even behavioral factors can prove fatal to the species.

3

Evolution of the ability to respond to *changes* in the environment clearly added a new dimension to the capacity of organisms to adapt. Specialized physiological responses such as the growth of plants toward light and hibernation of some mammals in cold weather provide for some adjustment to environmental changes. However, the most flexible basis of individual adaptation was provided by evolution of the capacity of the individual organism to vary its behavioral responses in terms of different environmental requirements—that is, to learn. Learning can do quickly what evolution can do only slowly. Whereas adaptation to a single environmental condition takes generations to achieve through evolution, an organism that can learn is able to tailor its own behavior to fit a variety of environmental conditions. Of course the ability to learn provides the basis for adaptation, but not all learning is adaptive. Just as effective behavior can be learned, so ineffective or neurotic behavior can also be learned.

For years psychologists and other biological scientists have attempted to develop a general definition of learning. Learning is most often defined as a more or less permanent change in behavior produced by experience. Although this is a useful working definition, it is admittedly imprecise. We will not have an adequate definition of learning until we know more about the varieties of behavioral plasticity that are considered examples of learning. For example, we use the phrase, "more or less permanent" as a hedge, because we do not yet know whether all the effects of experience are permanent. Certainly we and the other animals forget, and until we completely understand the nature of forgetting we cannot be certain whether, in the legendary words of William James, "nothing we ever do is, in strict scientific literalness, wiped out" [James, 1890, p. 127].

In analyzing behavior it is difficult to sort out the various influences which cause behavior to change. Learning does not take place in a vacuum, and the basic problem lies in distinguishing learning from other influences on behavior, such as fatigue, sensory adaptation, disease, injury, aging, and genetic contributions to the development of responses. For centuries man has trained animals of many species, including his own, by reward and punishment, or *instrumental conditioning*. A number of years ago two psychologists, Breland and Breland, developed a program of instrumental learning to train animal acts for county fairs and amusement parks. In general they were quite successful, but they encountered some interesting difficulties. For example, they trained a pig to pick up wooden coins and deposit them in a large "piggy bank" by rewarding it for successful responses [Breland and Breland, 1961, p. 683]:

At first the pig would eagerly pick up one dollar, carry it to the bank, run back, get another, . . . and so on. . . . Thereafter, over a period of weeks the behavior would become slower and slower. He might run over eagerly for each dollar, but on the way back, instead of carrying the dollar and depositing it simply and cleanly, he would repeatedly drop it, root it [that is, push it with his nose], drop it again, root it along the way, pick it up, toss it up in the air, drop it, [and] root it some more.

This pattern persisted even when the pig became extremely hungry because it worked too slowly to get enough to eat over the course of the day. Why did the learned behavior deteriorate? Breland and Breland suggested that the rooting behavior competed with the learned behavior because rooting is built into this species as part of the food-getting repertoire. On the basis of many similar observations with various other species, they reached the important conclusion that "the behavior of any species cannot be adequately understood, predicted, or controlled without knowledge of its institutional patterns, evolutionary history and ecological niche" [Breland and Breland, 1961, p. 684]. This point has bearing on many of the aspects of learning we shall discuss.

It is often assumed that only one or perhaps two forms of behavioral modification can properly be called learning. It is becoming increasingly apparent, however, that there are a number of types of behavioral modifications produced by experience. A complete understanding of learning must be based on an examination of each type. There is reason to believe that much of the variety simply reflects differences in the training procedures. However, there may well be actual differences in the neurobiological mechanisms of some types of learning.

## HABITUATION

One form of learning observed in all species, from the single-celled protozoan to man, is *habituation*, the decrease in response to a specific stimulus with repeated stimulation. When we hear an unexpected noise our attention is aroused and directed toward its source. If the noise is repeated, we habituate to it; we cease paying attention to it and eventually may not even be aware of it. For example, as we sit by a highway we often quickly come to ignore the sounds of passing automobiles. Responsiveness to repeated stimulation can decrease for other reasons which we must be careful to distinguish from habituation. In habituation the decrease in responsiveness is fairly specific to a particular stimulus. Following habituation of a response to a specific stimulus the response can still be elicited by stimuli other than the specific one to which it was habituated. This is in contrast to *sensory adaptation*, which affects sensitivity to all stimuli within a given sensory modality. Habituation must also be differentiated from *fatigue*, which decreases responsiveness to *all* stimulation. Under some circumstances repeated stimulation can also lead to increased responsiveness, or *sensitization*. However, the increased responsiveness is not necessarily

**5**

TABLE 1-1 *Average number of trials required for habituation in spirostomum to mechanical stimulation repeated at 5-minute intervals [Applewhite, 1968].*

|  | AVERAGE NO. OF TRIALS |
|---|---|
| Whole naïve animals | 9.0 |
| Halves of habituated animals |  |
| Anterior | 3.1 |
| Posterior | 3.6 |
| Halves of naïve animals |  |
| Anterior | 7.1 |
| Posterior | 9.6 |

stimulus specific. Habituation is often termed the simplest form of behavioral plasticity. It is obviously an adaptive function, and it is possible that the evolution of altered responsiveness in simple animals may have provided a basis of subsequent evolution of more complex learning processes.

Several examples will illustrate the pervasiveness of habituation. The protozoan *spirostomum* responds to stimulation by contracting. Applewhite [1968] found that when these single-celled animals were repeatedly stimulated by a mild jarring vibration every 5 seconds their response progressively decreased. In one experiment the animals ceased all contractions after only nine jarrings. After training the animals were cut in half, and the two sections (anterior and posterior) were given additional habituation training. Rehabituation of the severed halves took fewer than four trials (see Table 1-1). When naïve animals were cut in half the sections habituated in approximately the same number of trials as the intact animals (7 to 10 trials). Further tests showed that the decrease in responsiveness was not due either to fatigue or to local sensory adaptation. Clearly habituation in simple organisms does not require an organized nervous system.

Habituation of responses, including responses to socially significant stimuli, has been studied extensively in more complex species [Thorpe, 1963]. According to Lorenz [1969], wildfowl react to the approach of a furry animal such as a dog at the edge of their pond by escaping and "cautious mobbing" of the animal. However, birds that remain in the same region become habituated to specific dogs—that is, their responsiveness to them decreases. This habituation is highly stimulus specific; the birds respond readily when a strange dog wanders into the area. Some of the clearest evidence of habituation is seen in fish. The male three-spined stickleback will defend its newly constructed nest by attacking other males which intrude into its territory [Tinbergen, 1951]. Peeke [1969] studied the habituation of these aggressive responses by placing either a wooden model of a male fish or a live male stickleback (restrained in a clear plastic tube) directly into an aquarium each day for

6

10 days. Figure 1-1 shows the decrease with repeated exposure in attacks on the "intruder." The live fish elicited many more responses than the model. Note that the biting response decreased during each day but that some recovery occurred between each pair of days, although the responsiveness clearly decreased over a 10-day period. As is the case with other forms of behavioral plasticity, habituation is frequently short-lasting, as it is with the protozoan discussed above, and under other circumstances it can be quite persistent.

It is generally, and no doubt properly, assumed that in multi-cellular animals the plasticity underlying learning is due to changes in neural tissue. There is considerable controversy over whether learning can occur in restricted portions of the nervous systems of vertebrates, particularly in the spinal cord. Research by Thompson has provided conclusive affirmative evidence [Thompson, 1967; Thompson and Spencer, 1966; Groves and Thompson, 1970]. Habituation of a flexion response to repeated stimulation was obtained in laboratory animals in which the spinal cord had been surgically severed from the brain. The stimulus was a shock applied to the animal's skin and the response was a muscle contraction. The amplitude of the response decreased with stimulus repetition, recovered with time, and was then readily rehabituated. The electrical activity of nerve cells within the spinal cord, termed *interneurons*, was recorded by means of microelectrodes during habituation trials (see Fig. 1-2). Interestingly, three types of cells were found—cells which showed no changes in frequency of firing with repetition, cells which initially showed increased activity with repetition, and cells which showed decreased activity with repetition. The three types of cells are referred to as type *N* (nonplastic), type *H* (habituation), and type *S* (sensitization). In addition to differing in frequency of firing with repeated stimulation, the cells differ in their speed of response

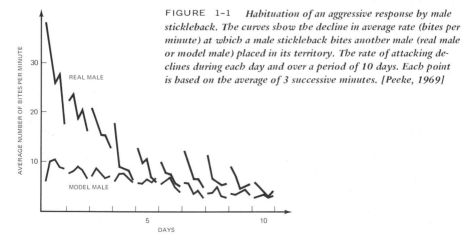

FIGURE 1-1   *Habituation of an aggressive response by male stickleback. The curves show the decline in average rate (bites per minute) at which a male stickleback bites another male (real male or model male) placed in its territory. The rate of attacking declines during each day and over a period of 10 days. Each point is based on the average of 3 successive minutes. [Peeke, 1969]*

LEARNING

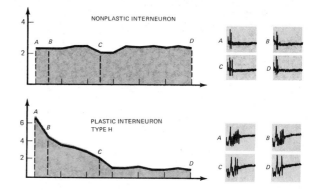

FIGURE 1–2 *Three types of spinal interneurons. The curves show responsiveness to sensory stimulation (mean number of spikes per stimulus) with increasing number of trials. A through D on the right of each curve show the electrical response of a typical cell— A before habituation, B on the first several trials, C after a number of trials, and D at the end of the*

following stimulation. Furthermore, the different types of cells are located in different regions of the spinal cord. Neurons in this phylogenetically old region of the nervous system appear to be specialized for different types of responses to stimulation.

These findings are not too surprising in view of the evidence that habituation can occur even in single-celled animals. Analysis of the features of single cells which make such plasticity possible may lead to an understanding of the neurobiological bases of more complex forms of learning—but again, this is a complex and controversial issue. Some of the reasons for the controversy will become clear as we consider other forms of learning which have been studied in man and the other animals.

## CLASSICAL AND INSTRUMENTAL CONDITIONING

Although animal training has been practiced for many centuries and naturalistic observations of learning have been made by scholars since recorded history, experimental studies of learning began only in the latter part of the last century. Ebbinghaus' classical research on memory was published in 1885. The Russian physiologist Pavlov and the American psychologist Thorndike both began laboratory studies of learning in animals just at the turn of the century. For decades the research and writings of these pioneer investigators were dominant influences in the development of theories and experimental analyses of learning. Many contemporary techniques, problems, and theories stem directly from these influences.

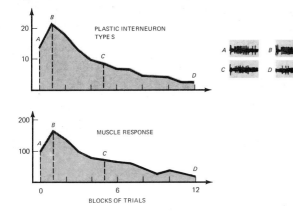

PLASTIC INTERNEURON TYPE S

MUSCLE RESPONSE

BLOCKS OF TRIALS

*habituation session. In nonplastic interneurons responsiveness does not change with repeated stimulation. In plastic type-H interneurons responsiveness decreases with stimulation. In plastic type-S interneurons responsiveness first increases, and then habituates. [Groves and Thompson, 1970]*

## CLASSICAL PAVLOVIAN CONDITIONING

The methods used by Pavlov in his studies of conditioning in dogs were based on his earlier work on the physiology of digestion (for which he was awarded the Nobel prize in 1904). Some of his basic findings are common knowledge. When meat powder is placed on a dog's tongue, the dog salivates. If some other stimulus, such as a bell or sound of a ticking metronome, is presented along with the meat powder on several occasions, the other stimulus will eventually elicit salivation when presented without the food. The process of pairing the meat powder with the bell is termed *reinforcement*. The stimulus which elicits the response is termed the *unconditioned stimulus*, and the initial response is called the *unconditioned response*. The signal is referred to as the *conditioned stimulus* and the learned response is called the *conditioned response*. An essential feature of this *classical* conditioning procedure is that the conditioned stimulus and unconditioned stimulus are controlled by the experimenter; the dog has no control over the delivery of the meat powder. The speed of acquisition of the conditioned response in classical conditioning is influenced by many factors. One of the most important of these is the time at which the conditioned stimulus is presented. Optimal conditioning occurs when the conditioned stimulus terminates shortly (0.5 second) before the onset of the unconditioned stimulus. Conditioning probably does not occur when the unconditioned stimulus precedes the conditioned stimulus.

Pavlov also observed a number of other interesting phenomena, which are summarized in Fig. 1-3. After conditioning, if the conditioned stimulus is presented alone, the response will decrease, or *extinguish*. In

**9**

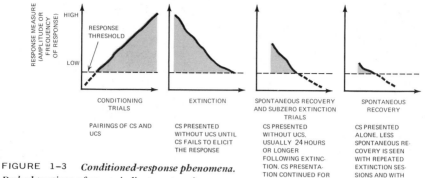

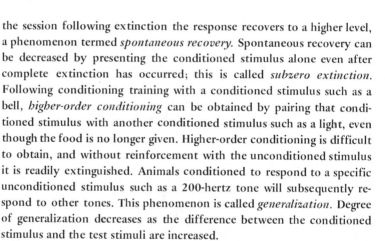

| CONDITIONING TRIALS | EXTINCTION | SPONTANEOUS RECOVERY AND SUBZERO EXTINCTION TRIALS | SPONTANEOUS RECOVERY |
|---|---|---|---|
| PAIRINGS OF CS AND UCS | CS PRESENTED WITHOUT UCS UNTIL CS FAILS TO ELICIT THE RESPONSE | CS PRESENTED WITHOUT UCS, USUALLY 24 HOURS OR LONGER FOLLOWING EXTINCTION. CS PRESENTATION CONTINUED FOR A NUMBER OF TRIALS FOLLOWING EXTINCTION. | CS PRESENTED ALONE. LESS SPONTANEOUS RECOVERY IS SEEN WITH REPEATED EXTINCTION SESSIONS AND WITH SUBZERO EXTINCTION. |

FIGURE 1–3  *Conditioned-response phenomena. Dashed portions of curves indicate responsiveness which is below the threshold for the measurable response.*

the session following extinction the response recovers to a higher level, a phenomenon termed *spontaneous recovery.* Spontaneous recovery can be decreased by presenting the conditioned stimulus alone even after complete extinction has occurred; this is called *subzero extinction.* Following conditioning training with a conditioned stimulus such as a bell, *higher-order conditioning* can be obtained by pairing that conditioned stimulus with another conditioned stimulus such as a light, even though the food is no longer given. Higher-order conditioning is difficult to obtain, and without reinforcement with the unconditioned stimulus it is readily extinguished. Animals conditioned to respond to a specific unconditioned stimulus such as a 200-hertz tone will subsequently respond to other tones. This phenomenon is called *generalization.* Degree of generalization decreases as the difference between the conditioned stimulus and the test stimuli are increased.

These are some of the major phenomena studied by Pavlov. In numerous experiments, by Pavlov as well as other investigators, many stimuli have been used as conditioned stimuli, many responses other than salivation have been studied, and other stimuli, such as electric shock, have been used as unconditioned stimuli.

What conclusions can be drawn about classical conditioning? Pavlov regarded conditioning as the fundamental process of association and regarded the conditioning experiments as providing a means of investigating the mechanisms of brain functioning underlying complex behavior. According to Pavlov [1957, pp. 197–198]:

The conditioned reflex is a common and widespread phenomenon. It is, evidently, what we recognize in ourselves and in animals under such names as training, discipline, education, habits; these are nothing but connections established in the course of individual existence, connections between definite external stimuli and corresponding reactions. Thus the conditioned reflex opens to the physiologist the door to investigation of a considerable part, and possibly, even of the entire higher nervous activity.

Other investigators have regarded classical conditioning as one of two, or perhaps several, types of learning. However the facts of conditioning are interpreted, it is clear that classical conditioning is a specific method of training animals. In view of this, some of the phenomena obtained with classical conditioning may differ from those obtained with other methods. However, it seems likely that the neurobiological bases of classical conditioning do not differ fundamentally from those of other forms of learning. It is sometimes assumed that classical conditioning consists only of training an animal to make a specific conditioned response, say salivation, to a specific stimulus, say a 200-hertz tone, and that the conditioned response is identical to the unconditioned response [Pavlov, 1957]. If this were true, we would need only to understand how a conditioned stimulus can substitute for an unconditioned stimulus in order to explain conditioning. The facts of conditioning are somewhat different from this concept. Zener reported his experiments in using a bell as a conditioned stimulus and salivation as an unconditioned response [1937, p. 393] :

> Except for the component of salivary secretion the conditioned and unconditioned behavior is not identical. The *CR* [conditioned response] . . . is a different reaction from the *UCR* [unconditioned response] anthropomorphically describable as looking, expecting, the fall of food with a readiness to perform the eating behavior which will occur when the food falls. The effector pattern is not identical with the *UCR* [unconditioned response].

Another more complex and interesting observation was made by Liddell while he was working in Pavlov's laboratory. A dog which had been conditioned to salivate at the acceleration of the beat of a metronome was freed from its harness. As reported by Lorenz [1969, p. 47] :

> The dog at once ran to the machine, wagged its tail at it, tried to jump up to it, barked, and so on; in other words, it showed as clearly as possible the whole system of behavior patterns serving, in a number of *canidae*, to beg food. . . . It is, in fact, this whole system that is being conditioned in the classical experiment.

Obviously when animals are trained with classical conditioning procedures they learn much more than the specific response which is measured during the training. This is one of the basic facts of learning which has made it difficult to develop an adequate general theory of learning. It is relatively easy to control behavior through training. However, it is not easy to specify the nature of the changes produced by the training.

## INSTRUMENTAL CONDITIONING

The learning obtained with reward-and-punishment training procedures, termed *instrumental conditioning*, was first studied by Thorndike during his graduate work under William James. These studies, like Pavlov's, were

11

begun just before the turn of the century. Thorndike placed laboratory animals, usually cats, in a small cage which could be opened, providing escape and a food reward, only if the cats made a specific response such as turning a latch or pulling a string. On the first few trials the animals made a variety of responses prior to making the "correct" one. As training continued, the irrelevant, or "incorrect," responses decreased, and the animals escaped within a short time after being placed in the problem box [Thorndike, 1932]. These procedures are, of course, the same as those we use to train our dog to "shake hands" or "roll over." In instrumental conditioning, in contrast to classical conditioning, the animal's behavior is "instrumental" in influencing the consequences of behavior; the reward is not given, or the punishment is not avoided, unless the animal makes the appropriate response. The environmental consequences—rewards and punishments—"select" adaptive responses, and the behavior of individual animals can thus become shaped to the requirements of the environment. From the animal's standpoint learning enables it to gain some degree of control over its environment.

In the artificial environment of the laboratory animals have been taught an enormous variety of responses. Instrumental-conditioning procedures have been successfully used to teach tricks to animals. Instrumental conditioning is also referred to as *operant conditioning*. This term was introduced by Skinner [1938], who also developed the well-known training apparatus—called the Skinner box—in which animals are given a small reward, or *reinforcement*, for pressing a lever. This technique enables us to study the effects of various rewards and other influences on the rate of response and has provided a means of investigating such things as sensory processes in animals. For example, an animal can be taught to press a lever only in the presence of a particular stimulus, and by varying the stimulus intensity, its sensory threshold for that stimulus can be measured. Studies of instrumental, or operant, conditioning have also revealed a number of interesting phenomena not observed in classical conditioning. For example, the pattern of responding is influenced by the frequency and pattern of rewards. Rewards can be given after each response, or they can be given only intermittently—that is, after either a fixed or random number of responses or after a fixed or random interval. Examples of the effects of different schedules of reward are shown in Fig. 1-4.

Operant conditioning in which response rate is the critical observation should be regarded as a special variety of instrumental conditioning. Most kinds of instrumental-learning tasks use measures of the time required for a response or of the number of errors made with repeated trials. A variety of other procedures are used in studies of instrumental learning. They all employ reward or punishment to induce animals to respond or stop responding (inhibitory avoidance). In some cases the response may produce a reward, and in others it may lead to the escape from or avoidance of a punishing stimulus. Each procedure produces a different type of behavioral modification—but all these procedures result in learning.

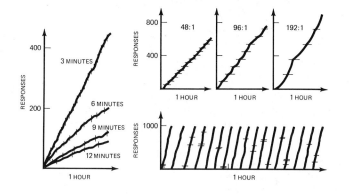

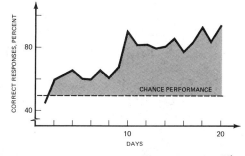

FIGURE 1-4 *Cumulative-response curves obtained with various schedules of rewards. Lines through the curves indicate delivery of reward. Left, fixed interval, the cumulative responses over a 1-hour period when rats are rewarded for the first lever pressing response made after 3, 6, 9, or 12 minutes. Center, fixed ratio, the cumulative responses of rats rewarded for every 48, 96, or 192 responses. Right, variable interval, the cumulative pecking responses of a pigeon rewarded at intervals ranging from 10 seconds to 21 minutes, with an average of five rewards per hour. Note that the rate of response varies with the type of reward schedule used. [Skinner, 1938; 1950]*

FIGURE 1-5 *Visual-discrimination learning by monkeys for visual exploration reward. Correct responses were rewarded only by an opportunity to look at a complex visual stimulus. [Butler, 1953]*

For some years researchers attempted to see whether events which are rewarding and punishing, termed *reinforcements*, might have a common basis. For example, Hull [1943] proposed that reinforcements act by decreasing biological drives such as hunger and thirst, and that such reinforcement was essential for learning to occur. One difficulty with this view is that an enormous variety of stimuli can act as reinforcers, that is, modify performance—and many appear to be unrelated to drives such as hunger and thirst. Animals will work for such rewards as variation in sensory stimulation. Neither beast nor man works for bread alone. Some examples of the reward effects of various visual stimuli are shown in Fig. 1-5.

The story is told of the researcher who, curious to find out what laboratory monkeys do when they are not being observed by psychol-

**13**

ogists, peeked through a laboratory door keyhole, only to see a monkey's eye peeking back at him. Harlow has shown that monkeys will press a lever for hours just for the opportunity to peek at an electric train, the laboratory room outside their chamber, or even the experimenter, and will solve problems when the only reward is the working of the problem or whatever satisfaction results from its solution [Harlow and McClearn, 1954; Butler, 1954b]. Humans, of course, engage in countless intellectual, athletic, and esthetic activities which are not rooted in the satisfaction of needs essential to life.

A number of years ago Olds and Milner [1954] discovered that laboratory rats could be trained to perform instrumental tasks such as pressing levers and even running mazes when the only reward was a small amount of electric current delivered directly to their brains. This remarkable discovery has been substantiated in extensive subsequent research, and demonstrations of the rewarding effects of intracranial stimulation are now commonplace. This finding also dramatically stimulated interest in the neural bases of motivation and learning.

Rewarding behavior by electrical stimulation of the brain has become a useful technique in examining possible differences between classical and instrumental learning. For example, it was long thought that responses controlled by the autonomic nervous system were modified only by classical conditioning, while skeletal responses controlled by the central nervous system were modified through instrumental conditioning. However, in a series of elegant studies Miller et al. have shown that such autonomic functions as heart rate and intestinal contractions can be modified by instrumental conditioning (see Fig. 1-6). After temporarily paralyzing rats with curare, which paralyzes the skeletal

FIGURE 1-6 *Instrumental conditioning of autonomic responses in rats. Left, effects on heart rate of rewarding increases or decreases in heart rate or in intestinal contraction. Right, effects on intestinal contraction of rewarding increases or decreases in intestinal contraction or in heart rate. Only the response specifically rewarded is modified by the reward. Intracranial electrical stimulation was used as the reward, with the animals paralyzed by curare in order to eliminate skeletal responses. [Miller and Banuazizi, 1968]*

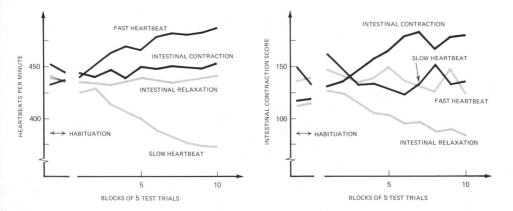

muscles without preventing autonomic responses, they placed electrodes into "rewarding" areas of the rats' brains and administered electrical stimulation whenever heart rate changed or degree of intestinal contractions altered. For some rats increases in autonomic responses were rewarded, while for others decreases were rewarded. The findings indicated that both responses were modified by the stimulation; the rates of autonomic responses could be either increased or decreased. Moreover, differential rewarding of one of the responses, such as heart rate, did not affect the other response, intestinal contraction. Comparable findings were obtained when the reward used was escape from mild electric shocks. Autonomically mediated responses are clearly influenced by instrumental conditioning procedures. Thus the contention that classical and instrumental conditioning have different neural bases is not borne out by the evidence.

In another interesting series of experiments Solomon et al. showed that a response learned through classical conditioning procedures can influence instrumental responses learned in the same situation [Maier et al., 1969; Rescorla and LoLordo, 1965]. In one study dogs were first trained to jump back and forth over a hurdle from one side of a shuttlebox to the other in order to avoid a foot shock. After the rate of response had stabilized at about six shuttles per minute, the dogs were given a series of classical conditioning trials in which one conditioned stimulus was followed by a foot shock and another conditioned stimulus was followed by no shock. The dogs were then tested in the shuttle box again. When the conditioned stimulus previously followed by a foot shock was presented, their shuttling rate increased dramatically; when the "safe" conditioned stimulus was presented, the rate of shuttling decreased. Clearly, the instrumentally conditioned behavior of the dogs' was markedly influenced by the *meaning* of the two conditioned stimuli, which was acquired during the classical-conditioning training.

Studies of classical and instrumental conditioning have demonstrated that virtually any discriminable stimulus can acquire meaning through its association with another meaningful stimulus. Stimuli followed by rewards and punishments can come to produce behavioral changes. In instrumental conditioning the experimenter can specify the nature of the response by making the delivery of reward or punishment contingent on the response. In classical conditioning the animal responds to a previously neutral conditioned stimulus even though it has no control over the delivery of the rewarding or punishing unconditioned stimulus. In both cases environmental stimuli acquire meaning.

Because of the robustness of the phenomena of classical and instrumental conditioning, the effectiveness of conditioning in controlling behavior has sometimes been overestimated. Furthermore, it is widely believed that any arbitrarily selected stimulus can become a cue for any rewards or punishments which it precedes. Pavlov proposed, for example, that "any natural phenomena chosen at will may be converted into 'conditioned stimuli' " [Pavlov, 1927]. However, some interesting recent discoveries limit this generalization. It is well known that rats which have survived poisoning subsequently avoid the *food* that poisoned them, but not the *place* where the food was located [Barnett, 1963]. What is the basis of this selective and highly adaptive behavior? In a series of experiments Garcia et al. [1968] found that rats will associate a general illness with something they have eaten (as though they responded with, "It must have been something I ate"). However, if they are given a painful stimulus such as an electric shock, they selectively avoid visual and auditory stimuli which preceded the punishment.

Apparently rats cannot learn to associate general illness with sights and sounds or to associate pain with food taste. In another experiment hungry rats were given either large or small food pellets which were coated with either powdered sugar or flour. Several groups of rats were given a painful foot shock every time they selected a pellet of a particular size or flavor. Rats in other groups were made ill by an x-ray treatment given immediately after the 1-hour period of eating pellets of a particular size and flavor. Two days later each group was tested to see whether the rats had learned to associate flavor and size with the two types of punishments. As Fig. 1-7 indicates, the animals given foot shocks readily ate pellets of either *flavor*, but they selectively avoided pellets of the *size* associated with foot shock. Rats given x-ray treatments readily ate pellets of either *size*, but they selectively avoided pellets of the *flavor* associated with the x-ray treatment. Garcia et al. concluded from these findings that pairing a perceptible cue with an effective reinforcer does not necessarily result in associative learning and that for a cue to be effective it must be related to the consequences that ensue.

An added point of interest is that the x ray was effective as a reinforcer and led to selective avoidance of a stimulus even though the animals did not become ill for some time after x-ray treatment. Although rewards and punishments are generally effective only when they are given either immediately or shortly after a training experience, delayed punishment in the form of general malaise is readily associated with food eaten some time earlier. The adaptive consequences of this ability provide stomachaches and security for the rat and ulcers and headaches for the farmer. It seems likely that the selectivity of associations between cues and consequences may be a fairly general phenomenon. Apparently anything cannot be made to stand for anything else as is often assumed.

## THE LEARNING AND PERFORMANCE OF RESPONSES

In one sense rewards and punishments are essential for instrumental learning; they clearly cause animals to perform, and they shape responses. Without rewards and punishments responses to stimuli usually extinguish or habituate. Rewards are essential to ensure the repetition of responses, but are they essential for learning to occur? According to Thorndike [1932], and later Hull [1943], rewards cause learning to occur. If this

**16**

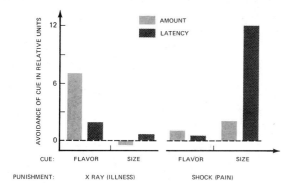

FIGURE 1–7    *Relative effectiveness of the size and flavor of food as cues when they are associated with either an electric shock or illness produced by x ray. When x ray is used as punishment the rats avoid foods with a particular flavor; the size of the food is not effective as a cue. When electric shock is used as punishment the rats avoid pellets of a particular size; flavor is not an effective cue. [Garcia et al., 1968]*

were true, of course, habituation and extinction, and perhaps even classical conditioning, could not be regarded as types of learning.

From another perspective, however, rewards and punishments control performance indirectly by influencing responses. According to this view, proposed by Tolman [1932], what is *learned* depends on the animal's sensory experiences, including the rewarding and punishing stimuli provided by the environment. What is *performed*, of course, depends not only on what has been learned, but also on the particular motivation of the animal when it is tested and the particular rewarding and punishing features of the environment. Thus a reinforced training trial provides an animal with the opportunity of learning about the environment—including, possibly, learning how to make a particular response. For example, if the reinforcement is irrelevant at the time, as when food is given to a satiated animal, the animal still may learn something about it even though there is no immediate behavioral response. A motivated animal may also have learned a great deal about its environment and not respond differentially in it until rewards are introduced to shape a specific response. Moreover, nearly all animals are capable at any given moment of performing any selection of an incredibly large number of previously learned responses, but what they do perform depends on the behaviors and motivations specific to their species.

There have been numerous studies of the effects of motivation on learning. Under some conditions performance varies with level of motivation, but this is not always the case, particularly when the response measure is errors rather than speed of response. In one interesting experiment Miles [1959] studied the effect of varying the length of food deprivation on discrimination learning in squirrel monkeys. In discrimination learning animals are taught to respond selectively to particular cues or objects. For example, an animal may be rewarded for choosing a black object presented along with objects which are white or grey. The monkeys were trained on both an easy and a difficult discrimination

**17**

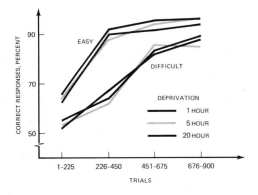

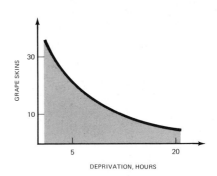

FIGURE 1-8 *Effects of degree of food deprivation and task difficulty on discrimination learning in monkeys. Deprivation did not affect performance on either the easy or the difficult task but did affect food motivation. Willingness to eat the grape skins increased with hours of food deprivation.* [Miles, 1959]

task. Each monkey was trained under three food-deprivation conditions—1 hour, 5 hours, and 20 hours. As Fig. 1-8 shows, the deprivation conditions did not affect rate of learning, but they did produce differing degrees of motivation. Grapes were used as rewards. When the monkeys were deprived of food for 20 hours they ate the grapes skins and all. Under the 1-hour deprivation conditions they ate the meat of the grapes but spit the skins out on the floor, where they were counted.

Experimental studies of *latent*, or hidden, learning in rats have shown that performance and learning can and should be distinguished. In studies of latent learning animals are allowed to learn without rewards and are then given rewards to see whether their performance has been influenced by the nonrewarded training. For example, in one of the pioneering studies of latent learning Tolman and Honzik [1930] placed rats deprived of food and water in an alley maze once each day for 17 days. One group of rats was given a food reward each day when it reached the goal box, a second group was never rewarded, and a third group was not rewarded for the first 10 trials. On the eleventh trial and each subsequent trial this third group found food in the goal box. Figure 1-9 shows the average number of errors, the entrances into blind alleys in the maze, made by each group on each day. Over the 17 days the performance of the rewarded animals was clearly superior to that of the nonrewarded controls. This was to be expected, of course, since there was no particular reason for the animals to decrease their entrances into blind alleys, except as a result of habituation, or possibly, the mild punishing effect of being forced to turn around in a narrow alley. Clearly, however, the animals learned about the maze when they were not rewarded. On the last six days of the test the performance of

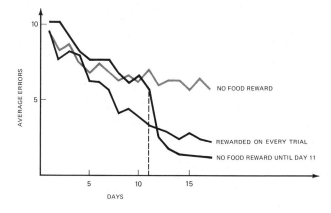

FIGURE 1–9 *Latent learning in rats. The rewarded group performed much better than the group that was never rewarded. The performance of a third group, not rewarded until the eleventh trial, was like that of the unrewarded group on the first 11 trials and like that of the consistently rewarded group (perhaps even better) on the last several trials; the latent learning was not apparent in performance until after the animals were given a rewarded trial. [Tolman and Honzik, 1930]*

the rats that had not found food in the goal box until trial 11 was even slightly superior to that of the animals that had been rewarded throughout the training.

This type of experiment has been successfully replicated many times. Although there is controversy over precise interpretation of the results, they strongly support the view that rewards do not directly influence learning. Furthermore these findings clearly indicate that learning must be distinguished from performance. Performance is influenced by many variables, and one important variable is what the animal has learned about its environment. The problem in defining learning, however, lies in distinguishing learning from the other variables that influence performance.

Thorpe [1963] has convincingly argued that latent learning is a basic capacity of many species, including insects. The digger wasp, for example, identifies its nest by the features peculiar to the terrain around it. As it leaves its nest the wasp may circle the area several times, suggesting that it is examining the terrain, and if salient landmarks are rearranged, it may subsequently be unable to locate the nest. Animals in their natural environments must be able to learn about the spatial relationships of important regions of their environments, such as food and water sources and the home or nest. If reward, such as the capture of prey, increases the probability that an animal will frequent a particular rotting log, brook, or meadow, the animal must be able to remember the location of that log, brook, or meadow. Laboratory training procedures provide highly useful data, but since the laboratory is an artificial environment, the findings must be interpreted in terms of the requirements of the animal's natural habitat.

**19**

Despite the customary emphasis on classical and instrumental conditioning, other forms, such as habituation and latent learning are at least equally pervasive and often equally efficient. It has been shown, for example, that cats and monkeys can learn from observing other animals [John, 1967]. Some years ago Herbert and Harsh [1944] placed cats in cages where they could watch other cats solve several instrumental-learning tasks. Some cats observed the entire training session on each task; other cats watched only the latter part of each session, by which time performance of the trained cats was rapid and skilled. When the observers were then trained on the tasks, both groups had benefited from their observations, but the best performance was obtained in the cats that had watched the entire training session. These cats had apparently profited from observing the errors as well as the correct responses made by the model cats. The extent of observational learning of the type outside of the laboratory is not known, but it seems reasonable to conclude that it plays an important role in the socialization of mammals.

We know from observing children, and from being observed by children, that observation learning provides a basis for imitation. This is one of the most extensively used techniques in teaching, particularly in teaching children. Most of the skills taught in school, as well as most of the habits and prejudices taught at home and in other social institutions, are based initially on observational learning and imitation. Instrumental learning provides the subsequent shaping of responses—that is, it determines what responses will be made and how well they will be made—but observational learning and imitation provide the opportunity for instrumental learning to occur. The learning of language by humans and the learning of songs by birds are perhaps the clearest examples. Many species of birds learn specific songs from the adults of their species by listening and imitating. White-crowned sparrows normally acquire the full song during their first two years of life. Young birds that are isolated from adults fail to develop the particular dialect of adults from the same region. In white-crowned sparrows reared in the laboratory several months elapse between the time that the song pattern is acquired through listening and the time that birds produce the full song; the learning remains latent for several months until the birds start to sing. If the birds are deafened either before or even shortly after they are exposed to the adult song, their subsequent singing is abnormal. Apparently in order to translate the song patterns they have learned (through listening) into the full song, the birds must be able to hear themselves sing. Once the full song is developed, however, deafening has virtually no effect on subsequent singing [Konishi, 1965].

Earlier we noted that in classical conditioning an animal learns more than is revealed by the particular behavioral response it exhibits. This is also true for the various forms of instrumental learning. Thus the question of what is learned in any learning task cannot be answered completely by examining the specific response which is rewarded or punished. As a matter of fact, restricting attention to the response can lead to quite erroneous conclusions about the nature of learning. A number of years ago Liddell [1942] trained a sheep to avoid a shock to its foot by flexing its foreleg at the onset of a signal. After the response was well learned the sheep was placed on its back and the signal was presented. Under these conditions the sheep did not flex its foreleg. Instead it stiffened all four legs and attempted to lift its head. This was not the response it had learned through instrumental conditioning, but a completely different one which was in fact much more appropriate to the altered circumstances.

This example illustrates an extremely important point in relation to interpretations of classical and instrumental learning in complex animals. Even though a training procedure may elicit or require a specific response, the learning does not consist solely of an altered tendency to contract a specific set of muscles in a precise sequence in the presence of specific stimuli. Typically, we do not even study the response of the animal in a literal sense. Rather we study the *outcome* of responses—frequencies of lever presses, or number of errors versus correct turns in a maze, or even speed or probability of response. Since responses are rarely, if ever, made more than once in precisely the same way, it is not surprising to find that even in any given restricted environment an animal may learn to make a variety of responses which are collectively regarded by the experimenter as "a response." Furthermore, as we have seen, an animal may learn about features of the task in ways that enable him to perform "the response," when necessary, in ways that he has never previously performed it.

The report of Liddell's sheep is only one of numerous examples of this phenomenon. For example, Tolman et al. [1946] showed that rats could learn to go to the same place in a maze for a reward even though they had to make different turning responses on successive trials. On the basis of these findings they argued that such learning is based on the acquisition of a disposition to go to a particular place rather than to make a specific response or set of responses. In one study animals did develop specific turning responses, tendencies to turn right or left, with extensive training [Ritchie et al., 1950]. When the highly trained turning response was then interrupted by introducing a 3-inch gap in the floor at the point where a turn was required, the animals hesitated and then went to the previously rewarded *place* in the maze. Thus interference with the response "habit" once again allowed the place "disposition" to determine alley choices. Even when an animal is well trained to make what the experimenter regards as a specific response, it is capable of making other responses, even novel ones, which indicates that it has learned more than a specific response.

One of the most dramatic examples of the plasticity of learned responses was reported a number of years ago by Lashley and McCarthy [1926]. Rats were first trained in a simple alley maze, and after they had learned the maze, the cerebellum of each animal was destroyed by surgery. Since the cerebellum plays an important role in controlling

**21**

bodily movements, their locomotor behavior was seriously impaired. When the animals recovered from the acute effects of the surgery and were able to move about in some fashion, they were again tested in the maze. Although they had great difficulty in walking, retention of their maze training was virtually unaffected. One of the rats with the most severe impairment of locomotor activity made no errors at all on the retention test.

We do not know how the nervous system functions to provide for the phenomenal plasticity of learned responses. The adaptive advantages of this capacity are obvious. If learning consisted only of the acquisition of precise *movements* in the presence of specific stimuli, such a capacity would be of little adaptive value in a complex and changing environment.

## IMPRINTING

The complex nature of learning is seen in the rather special form of learning termed *imprinting* [Lorenz, 1937]. Under natural conditions the young of many species develop strong attachments to their parents. The brood of ducklings following their mother is a familiar example. This kind of attachment, or imprinting, develops during an early period in the animal's life. In a sense it is only accidental that the young become attached to their mother, since they will readily imprint on any salient object available during the early critical period. Ordinarily the mother duck is the most salient object in the duckling's early environment. Thus imprinting serves the important adaptive function of assuring with some probability that the duckling will stay close by its mother.

Systematic observations of imprinting were first made by Spalding [1873], who noted that newly hatched chicks would follow *any* moving object and had no more tendency to follow a hen than to follow a duck or even a human figure.

Subsequent research clearly confirms Spalding's observations; young birds can be imprinted to a great variety of objects. For example, Hess [1957] exposed chicks to a moving colored disk for a brief period. When the chicks were tested the following day they tended to follow that particular disk in preference to other disks they had not previously seen. Hess also studied the effectiveness of various types of stimuli in producing imprinting and found that a round ball (with structures resembling wings and a tail attached) was more effective than various objects which resemble an adult chicken. Somewhat surprisingly, a stuffed leghorn rooster was the least effective stimulus of all those tested. Complex moving objects are typically used in laboratory studies of imprinting, but birds will apparently imprint to almost any salient perceptual stimulus [Sluckin, 1965]. In natural environments young birds are likely to be imprinted on stimuli that aid in their survival. There is evidence

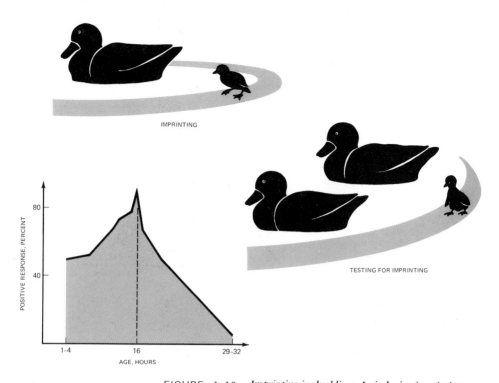

IMPRINTING

TESTING FOR IMPRINTING

FIGURE 1–10    *Imprinting in ducklings. In inducing imprinting the duckling is placed behind a model of a male duck which moves and makes sounds. The duckling is then placed between a female model and the male model used for imprinting, and the choice of the male is used as a measure of imprinting. The curve shows variation in effectiveness of imprinting as the duckling ages. Maximum effectiveness is found at 16 hours. [Hess, 1957]*

that naïve young chicks and ducklings have marked and stable preferences for the parental calls of their own species [Gottlieb, 1965]. These preferences increase the likelihood that the birds will imprint on members of their own species. Unfortunately it is also possible for birds to become imprinted on dangerous objects such as predators. Such birds are unlikely to become ancestors.

In chicks and ducklings the critical, or most sensitive, period for imprinting is the first day or after hatching (see Fig. 1-10). This sensitive period can be extended by restricting the visual environment for a day or two after hatching [Moltz and Stettner, 1961]; thus it is not determined completely by biological age. The sensitive period no doubt varies considerably in different species, probably in relation to the maturation rate of the particular species. There is some evidence that imprinting occurs in mammals including guinea pigs and sheep, although the evidence is much less convincing than that based on studies of chicks and ducklings.

Some of the most interesting effects of imprinting are seen in later social behavior, including courtship and mating. Numerous examples of

**23**

inappropriate or abnormal social behavior produced by imprinting have been described by Lorenz [1957, p. 146]:

A musk drake [*Cairina moschata*] hatched with four siblings by a pair of grey geese, and led by them for seven weeks, subsequently proved to be bound to his siblings, that is, to his own species, in all his social activities. But when his mating reactions awoke the following year, they were focussed on the species of the foster parents, to whom he had paid no attention for over ten months.

Frequently animals reared by scientists and zookeepers later court and attempt to mate with human beings rather than their own species. In the zoo in Basel, Switzerland, a tame emu regularly attempted to mate with its keeper during the mating season. Smaller animals may become attached to just the leg or shoe of the keeper [Hediger, 1950]. One of the strangest cases of mismating occurred at the Schönbrunn Zoo in Vienna, where a peacock was reared with giant Galápagos tortoises [Heinroth and Heinroth, 1959]. Clearly imprinting is not always adaptive.

In normally developed social attachments it is not always clear whether or not some sort of reward might have been a factor. In its purest form imprinting is not thought to be influenced by rewards or punishments. Nevertheless, a stimulus on which an animal has been imprinted can serve as a reward in instrumental learning [James, 1959; Campbell and Pickleman, 1961]. For example, in one study ducklings which were imprinted on a yellow cylinder were readily trained to peck at a disk which, when pressed, presented the yellow cylinder. Furthermore, the response did not extinguish even after the chicks made a large number of responses [Peterson, 1960].

Imprinting is clearly a form of learning and has a profound influence on later social life, including choice of a mate. The effects of the early imprinting experiences are thought to be lasting and at least partially irreversible. It is not yet clear, however, that imprinting is fundamentally different from other types of learning.

## COMPLEX LEARNING

In the types of learning discussed so far—habituation, classical and instrumental conditioning, and imprinting—we have focused on procedures which are used in a restricted environment to teach animals to make responses to a fairly restricted range of stimuli. Let us briefly consider learning in tasks where the responses are less controlled by the particular features of the stimulation. Through the use of rewards and/or punishments animals can be trained to discriminate—that is, to respond differentially to different stimuli. For example, if a rat is repeatedly rewarded for entering the darker of two alleys, it will learn to discriminate between the two alleys. The rat can then be taught

24

a discrimination reversal—that is, to choose the lighter of the two alleys. Initially, reversal learning will be a more difficult task. However, if the animal is taught a series of discrimination reversals, the rate of learning of each reversal increases, that is, it shows increasing profit from previous experiences (see Fig. 1-11). Under some conditions reversal learning can be improved by overtraining on the first discrimination. One interpretation of this effect is that through training with specific stimuli the animal comes to attend more readily to the particular stimuli involved rather than to other features of the training environment [Mackintosh, 1969].

Improvement in learning with training—learning to learn—has been extensively studied in primates by Harlow [1949a]. Monkeys subjected to prolonged discrimination training develop what has been termed *learning sets*—that is, they become increasingly skilled at solving discrimination learning tasks. They show improved learning not only of previously learned discriminations, but also of novel problems (see Fig. 1-12). Obviously the development of such learning sets frees them from the restrictions of the slow trial-and-error process of the original learning attempts. Through training experiences of this type monkeys can be taught highly complicated tasks, such as choosing the odd stimulus from an array of stimuli or choosing a stimulus which matches one displayed by the experimenter. Clearly much of the intellectual capacity of an individual animal depends on his previous learning experiences. The capacity for learning to learn provides even the monkey with a considerable degree of "intellectual freedom."

The most complex learning occurs in language development. The ability of the protozoan *spirostomum* to habituate to repeated stimulation seems trivial in comparison to the ability of the human child to learn to speak the language of its elders. Both phenomena, of course,

FIGURE 1–11 *Discrimination-reversal learning in monkeys. The monkeys are first taught to choose one object, and they are then rewarded for choosing the other object. The curve shows their performance on the second trial on successive block of 14 reversal problems. The animals have "learned to learn" to reverse their choices. [Harlow, 1949a]*

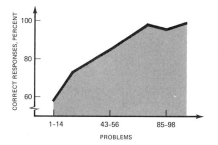

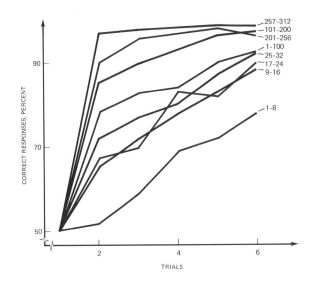

must be considered in terms of their adaptive significance for the species in question. Man is unique in the degree of his capacity to acquire and use language. Infrahumans can communicate in many ways, and the higher primates have exhibited a capacity for acquiring some of the rudiments of language. However, the linguistic achievements of apes are primitive in comparison to those of man.

The learning of language consists not only in acquisition of a vocabulary, but in acquisition of syntax, the rules of language that govern the order of words in sentences. These rules are learned early in life, and as we know from listening to people whose first language is not English, the syntax of the first-learned language will influence the syntax used in other languages acquired later. How do we learn the programs for responding that we call language? Clearly language is not learned through the instrumental conditioning of words or sentences. The readiness with which different words can be used to express the same thought and the way in which the same words can be used in different orders in a sentence argue strongly against such a simplistic view [Miller et al., 1960].

We do not know how the programs, or structures, that we call language are learned; what is clear, however, is that it is necessary for us to understand the bases of the learning of language before we will be able to completely understand the neurobiological bases of behavior.

Lashley [1951] once pointed out that the various problems raised by the organization of language are characteristic of almost all other cerebral activity. There is, for example, a serial ordering of the vocal movements involved in pronouncing the words in a sentence, the sentences in a paragraph, and the paragraphs in a longer discourse. All skilled acts appear to involve similar problems of serial ordering, even down to the coordination of muscular contractions in movements such as those of reaching and grasping. Thus investigation of the neural organization of the more simple motor skills may well provide important clues which will lead to an understanding of the neurobiological bases of language.

## VARIATIONS IN LEARNING CAPACITY

Not all species have the capacity to learn a language. Different species obviously differ in learning capacity, and individuals within a species differ because of such factors as genetic makeup, age, and learning history. It seems fairly certain that one form of learning, habituation, can be obtained in single-celled animals, although it is less certain, and even doubtful, that they are capable of other forms of learning [Jensen, 1965]. It is still not clear whether conditioning can occur in higher invertebrates such as planarians. Rather convincing findings of conditioning in planarians have been reported by McConnell [1966], but little or no evidence of it has been obtained in other studies, and it is often difficult to rule out other effects of training, such as sensitization.

Conditioning, including instrumental conditioning, is readily obtained, however, in mollusks and arthropods. Maze learning has been studied in ants as well as rats, and observational, or latent, learning appears to be common in many insects.

There have been a number of studies of learning in the cockroach, particularly in relation to restricted parts of neural tissue. The purpose of such studies is to find out what type of tissue will sustain learning and, if possible, something about the neural changes that underlie the learning. Learning in restricted regions of the mammalian nervous system (the spinal cord) was discussed above. Horridge [1965] has shown that cockroaches can learn even if their heads are removed. A subsequent study showed that learning could occur even when the response was mediated by only one ganglion (the prothoracic ganglion) [Eisenstein and Cohen, 1965]. A cockroach was attached to a rod, with its leg resting in a dish of water. The water was in a series with a shock source, so that the leg was shocked every time it touched the water. The

27

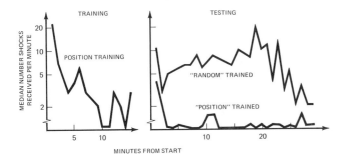

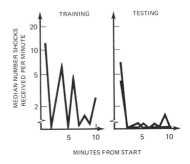

FIGURE 1-13 *Learning by a cockroach ganglion. Training and testing of position-trained and random-trained preparations. P leg received shock when a leg touched water. R leg received shock whenever P leg was shocked. Left curve shows decrease in shocks, with time, for P legs. Right curves show subsequent responses of P and R legs when both are given only P training. "Learning" by the R group was slower than original learning of P group. Below, training and testing of P and R legs in animals with ganglion removed.* [Eisenstein and Cohen, 1965]

learning consisted of holding the leg, designated the *P* leg, in a position that would keep it from touching the water. As a control the cockroach's other leg was given a shock whenever the *P* leg was shocked. Thus the *P* leg was shocked only when it was lowered into the water, while the control leg, termed *R* for random, was shocked in a variety of positions. Figure 1-13 shows the results. The *P* leg gradually learned to avoid the shock. When the *R* leg was subsequently trained, the earlier experience appeared to impair learning. Additional tests indicated that the learning did not consist merely in holding the leg in a fixed position. When the *P* leg was lowered slightly, so that the previously learned response would not avoid the shock, the animal (or ganglion) quickly relearned to avoid it even if a different type of response, extension rather than flexion, was required. Finally, as Fig. 1-13 shows, an avoidance response of some kind was also learned even if the leg was disconnected neurally from the ganglion, but such learning did not have the plasticity shown by the animals with an intact ganglion. Thus the plasticity of learning can be seen even in restricted portions of the nervous systems of infrahuman species of animals.

Vertebrate studies of learning have centered on the complexity of learning. As Fig. 1-14 shows, species differences in the formation of learning sets very roughly parallel evolutionary status. However, the bases of these differences are not yet known. In general it appears that species differ not simply in ability to learn, but in the complexity of the tasks they can learn to handle. Such differences are undoubtedly due to the evolution of neurobiological processes. Bitterman [1965] has

**28**

reported that some types of learning tasks, such as discrimination reversal learning, reveal systematic species differences among vertebrates. He suggests that the evolution of learning is not continuous, but rather that the more complex tasks tap a capacity that is present in higher animals but poorly developed in the turtle and absent in the fish; such differences might result from the evolution of brain structures, particularly the cerebral cortex. Whether these conclusions can be accepted will depend on subsequent research findings. However, since species differ in many features, including sensory and motivational processes, it may well be that species differences in behavior seen in such tasks are due to differences in processes other than those underlying learning.

The same caution holds for analyses of other differences in learning that are related to differences in biological factors. Bovet et al. [1969] have reported evidence of strain differences in avoidance learning and maze learning in various inbred strains of mice (see Fig. 1-15). There is fairly convincing evidence that strains which learn well in one task also learn well in the other, and that some strains are poor in both tasks. There may be some general factor underlying the consistent strain differences in learning, and it is tempting to conclude that they are due to genetically based differences in neurobiological processes. However, until such processes are identified, this conclusion remains inferential.

It is obvious that the learning capabilities of the young of many species are different from those of adults, and it is a common complaint, not without supporting evidence, that learning efficiency is decreased in the aged. The results of numerous studies of aging effects in learning generally support casual observation. For example, Oliverio and Bovet [1966] studied age differences in maze learning and avoidance learning in mice. In both tasks learning was least efficient in 21-day-old and 360-day-old mice and most efficient in 60-day-old mice. These age differences in learning were particularly striking when many training trials were given on each session. Harlow [1959a] conducted extensive studies

FIGURE 1-14 *Learning-set formation in different mammals. Curves show improvement on second trial in a large number of discrimination problems. Rhesus monkeys improve rapidly, rats and squirrels improve very slowly, and the performance of cats, marmosets, and squirrel monkeys is intermediate. [Warren, 1965]*

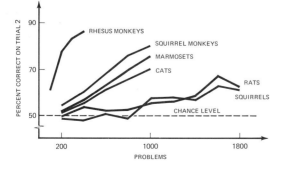

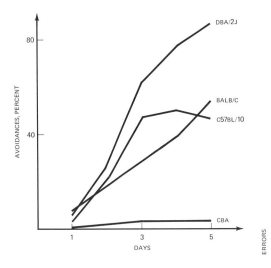

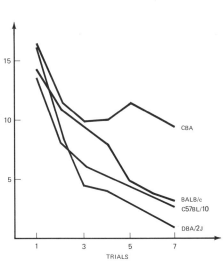

FIGURE 1–15    *Learning in four inbred strains of mice. Above, avoidance conditioning in a shuttle box. The animals were given 100 trials each day for five days. Right, maze learning. The animals were given one trial each day for 10 days. Note that strain CBA was worst on both tasks, while strain DBA/2J was superior on both tasks. [Bovet et al., 1969]*

FIGURE 1–16    *Improvement in discrimination learning with age in rhesus monkeys. Left, learning of a single discrimination problem as a function of age. Errors made in learning decrease with the age of the animals at the time that training began. Below, oddity learning. Monkeys learn to choose the object which differs from others in a set. Curves show performance on blocks of 64 problems, each 10 trials in length. Right, discrimination learning-set performance for training started at different ages compared to performance of an adult group. Curves show performance on trial 2 in a series of discrimination problems. [Harlow, 1959a]*

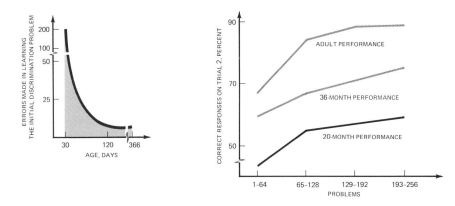

of age differences in learning in rhesus monkeys, with tasks which varied in complexity from a form of classical conditioning to learning-set formation. Simple classical conditioning was found even in neonatal monkeys. As Fig. 1-16 shows, the rate of learning of a simple discrimination problem increases with age up to about 150 days. However, in acquisition of learning sets 150-day-old monkeys are considerably inferior to year-old and adult monkeys. Finally, in oddity discrimination learning there are clear differences between twenty-month-old, three-year-old, and adult monkeys. No decline in performance was found with increasing age of the monkeys, but it was clear that the ability to learn tasks of varying complexity depends on the age of the animal [Harlow, 1959a, p. 478]:

> Early in life, new learning abilities appear rather suddenly within the space of a few days, but, from late infancy onward, the appearance of new learning powers is characterized by developmental stages during which particular performances progressively improve. There is a time at which increasingly difficult problems can first be solved, and a considerably delayed period before they can be solved with adult efficiency.

Although the effects of age in human learning have not been systematically studied, the available evidence is consistent with Harlow's findings on the effects in other primates. The general fact that at different ages humans are able to learn material of different complexity has considerable bearing on educational curricula. It is likely that the efficiency of the educational process could be dramatically improved if we knew more about the development of learning abilities in children. It is also well known that learning ability often declines in the aged. As yet, however, we know little about the neurobiology of either the development or the decline of learning ability.

We have discussed only a few of the important problems, concepts, and "facts" of learning. Since learning is a pervasive influence on behavior, it has dominated psychological research for the past century. The early ideas of pioneers such as Pavlov, Thorndike, and Tolman have stimulated research which has provided continuously increasing understanding of

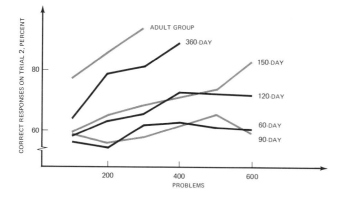

the way experiences shape our behavior. Nevertheless, there are still serious gaps in our knowledge of how experiences shape the behavior of man and other animals. We are only beginning to understand the highly complex processes of behavioral adaptation which we refer to collectively as learning, and as we acquire new information our understanding continues to change. As our understanding changes, so should our explicit use of the principles of learning in teaching and learning. As our knowledge increases we should become more effective in teaching our young to acquire the information and skills required by our society.

## SUMMARY

The survival of any species depends on its ability to adapt to special conditions of its environment and evolution of the capacity to learn provides a means for adaptation even to changing environments. Learning, a more or less permanent change in behavior produced by experience, is difficult to isolate from the multitude of other influences on behavior. However, several types of processes may generally be described as learning phenomena.

Habituation, a decrease in response to a repeated stimulus, and sensitization, an increase in response to a repeated stimulus, are perhaps the simplest forms of learning. Habituation, which occurs even in the single-celled *spirostomum*, is specific to a single stimulus and is not generalized to other stimuli within a stimulus mode. In classical, or Pavlovian, conditioning if two stimuli are paired, one of the pair will later elicit the response initially provoked by the other. Instrumental conditioning is the familiar technique of reward and punishment to elicit the appropriate response.

Although these simpler forms of conditioning have been studied at length, they fall short of explaining many phenomena of learning. In latent, or "hidden" learning, for example, animals learn without any observable reward. Furthermore, although conditioning procedures are employed to produce a specific response or specific groups of responses, the animal actually learns much more than that. Thus behavioral performance must be distinguished from what is learned in any learning situation. Other varieties of learning include imprinting on some salient stimulus during a critical period after birth and observational, or imitation learning, which is an important influence on the behavior of children. There are perhaps other forms of learning which we have not yet untangled from the many other influences that affect the behavior of organisms.

In addition to these simple varieties of learning, higher animals are capable of extremely complex forms of learning. Through the use of rewards and punishments they can be taught to make complex sensory discriminations. They can learn to reverse their initial responses, and they can learn to learn, a phenomenon termed learning set. The most complex of all learning, the learning of language, appears to be unique to man.

A fruitful approach to the analysis of learning is represented by the comparative description and analysis of learning capacities and possible neural mechanisms underlying various types of learning. Habituation and sensitization have been analyzed in even the simplest of organisms and conditioning is readily obtained in mollusks and arthropods. Comparison of the complex learning in various vertebrate species has provided a great deal of insight into the evolutionary and psychobiological mechanisms by which these differences arise.

# CHAPTER TWO

## THE MEMORY PROCESSES

Memory is quite clearly one of the most important capacities of man and the other animals. It is through memory that experiences of the past influence our present thoughts, plans, and actions. Without memory, of course, we would be unable to learn. It is difficult to imagine a human being lacking the ability to record experiences. Some signs of memory are usually seen even in the most severe cases of mental retardation. In the most general sense, memory refers to the lasting effect of stimulation—that is, the effect that remains after the stimulus is gone. As William James [1890] pointed out many years ago, "for a state of mind to survive in memory it must have endured for a certain length of time." We retain the influences of the experiences which occurred many years ago and we record the fleeting experiences of the moments just past. We remember our own telephone numbers and can report them at almost any time, but we remember a telephone number we have just looked up perhaps only long enough to dial it. What accounts for the wide variations in the lability or durability of memory?

Try to imagine what your life would be like if from this moment on you were unable to learn—unable to acquire any further information,

# MEMORY

attitudes, or skills—even though you could remember most of what you have learned up to this point. Some of the consequences of this disability are obvious; others may not be.

A disability of just this kind sometimes results from brain damage produced by disease, injury, and chronic nutritional deficiencies or from surgical removal of portions of the temporal lobes. Examination of a classical case will illustrate the dramatic effect of such surgery on the patient's memory [Milner, 1966, pp. 112–115]:

> "This young man (H.M.) . . . had had no obvious memory disturbance before his operation, having, for example, passed his high school examinations without difficulty. [He sustained] a minor head injury at the age of seven. Minor [seizures] began one year later, and then, at the age of 16, he began to have generalized seizures which, despite heavy medication, increased in frequency and severity until, by the age of 27, he was no longer able to work . . . ; his prospects were by then so desperate that the radical bilateral medial temporal lobe [surgery] . . . was performed. The patient was drowsy for the first few post-operative days but then, as he became more alert, a severe memory impairment was apparent. He could no longer recognize the hospital staff, apart from [the surgeon], whom he had known for many years; he did not remember and could not relearn the way to the bathroom, and he seemed to

retain nothing of the day-to-day happenings in the hospital. His early memories were seemingly vivid and intact, his speech was normal, and his social behaviour and emotional responses were entirely appropriate."

There has been little change in this clinical picture during the years which have elapsed since the operation. . . . there [is no] evidence of general intellectual loss; in fact, his intelligence as measured by standard tests is actually a little higher now than before the operation. . . . Yet the remarkable memory defect persists, and it is clear that H.M. can remember little of the experiences of the last . . . years. . . .

Ten months after the operation the family moved to a new house which was situated only a few blocks away from their old one, on the same street. When examined . . . nearly a year later, H.M. had not yet learned the new address, nor could he be trusted to find his way home alone, because he would go to the old house. Six years ago the family moved again, and H.M. is still unsure of his present address, although he does seem to know that he has moved. [The patient] . . . will do the same jigsaw puzzles day after day without showing any practice effect, and read the same magazines over and over again without finding their contents familiar. . . .

Even such profound amnesias as this are, however, compatible with a normal attention span. . . . On one occasion, he was asked to remember the number "584" and was then allowed to sit quietly with no interruption for 15 minutes, at which point he was able to recall the number correctly without hesitation. When asked how he had been able to do this, he replied,

"It's easy. You just remember 8. You see, 5, 8, and 4 add to 17. You remember 8; subtract it from 17 and it leaves 9. Divide 9 in half and you get 5 and 4, and there you are: 584. Easy."

In spite of H.M.'s elaborate mnemonic scheme he was unable, a minute or so later, to remember either the number "584" or any of the associated complex train of thought; in fact, he did not know that he had been given a number to remember. . . .

One gets some idea of what such an amnesic state must be like from H.M.'s own comments. . . . Between tests, he would suddenly look up and say, rather anxiously,

"Right now, I'm wondering. Have I done or said anything amiss? You see, at this moment everything looks clear to me, but what happened just before? That's what worries me. It's like waking from a dream; I just don't remember."

Similar symptoms have been found in other patients with damaged brains [Whitty and Zangwill, 1966]. Patients with this type of memory disorder are forced to live only in the immediate present, and as time goes on in the distant past. Since they lack the capacity to learn, they rely heavily on memories acquired before their disability developed. Generally their stock of old memories remains fairly intact. Such patients remember their native language, as well as others they may have learned in their youth. They may readily recite poems and remember old songs. They are able to perform skills and play games they learned earlier. However, they are unable to learn a new game, even though it is similar to others that they know well. As Barbizet has noted [1963, p. 128]:

> Such patients therefore who no longer fix the present live constantly in a past which preceded the onset of their illness. Their disengagement from the present is, however, far from complete. Some are conscious of the disorder of memory, like [one patient], who said: "When I watch closely I know, but I soon forget. My brain feels like a sieve, I forget everything. Even in my tiny room, I keep losing things. It all fades away."

These findings clearly suggest that we must distinguish between recent memories and older memories, and that different processes underlie each type. Why is it that the recent experiences of such patients do not leave lasting effects? What processes are affected by the brain damage? Some possible answers to these questions have been provided by findings of experimental studies of memory in animals and men. It is often the case in science that discovering what happens when something goes wrong can lead to an understanding of how a system works. Our current thinking about normal memory processes is strongly influenced by the information from studies in which memory functions have been modified either by accident or by design.

Evidence from a variety of sources, including the clinical findings cited above, suggests there may be several kinds of memory processes [McGaugh, 1966; 1968a; Drachman and Arbit, 1966]. A distinction between at least two processes, *short-term memory* and *long-term memory*, was proposed some time ago [Hebb, 1949; Gerard, 1949]. Nevertheless, some researchers believe that there is only one type of memory [Melton, 1963]. We do not yet have enough evidence to be certain which of these views is correct. There is no doubt, however, that the characteristics of recent memory differ in many ways from those of long-term memory.

## MEMORY AND IMAGES

If you look at a picture for a brief period and then look away, perhaps at a blank wall, you may be able to remember a great deal of the details of the picture for a short time. Later you will have forgotten many of the details even though you retain the ability to recognize the picture. Immediately after you look at the picture, however, you may feel that you have an image of it, and that this image is rapidly decaying. Studies of memory have provided rather strong support for the view that memory for very recent experiences is in fact imagelike. Two types of imagelike memory, iconic memory and eidetic imagery, have been extensively studied.

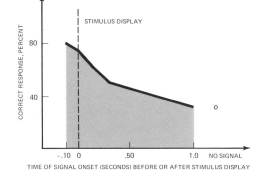

FIGURE 2–1 *Rapid decay of visual information. Twelve-item displays of numbers and figures (three rows of four items) were presented to subjects for 50 milliseconds. A tone signal was presented either before the display or at one of several intervals afterward. Open dot indicates average performance when no signal was given. [Sperling, 1960]*

## ICONIC MEMORY

*Iconic memory* is the very short-term imagelike memory evidenced by humans. Human subjects have almost perfect memory for items exposed briefly in a display if they are tested immediately afterward. In one study combinations of letters and numbers arrayed in two or three rows were exposed to subjects for 50 milliseconds [Sperling, 1960]. If the subjects were simply asked to report what they saw, they typically reported about four items correctly (out of a display containing 8 to 12 items). This is referred to as the *span of apprehension* or *immediate memory span.* In other tests a tone was sounded at intervals varying from 50 milliseconds before onset to 1 second following offset of the display. The pitch of the tone signaled which row of items the subject was to report; the highest tone was a signal to report the upper row and the lowest tone signaled the bottom row. The important feature of this test is that when the tone was presented afterward the subject could not tell which row he was to report until after the display was gone. Figure 2-1 shows typical results obtained from this experiment. If the tone was presented either immediately before or immediately after the exposure, accuracy was better than 80 percent. If the tone was delayed for 1 second after exposure, the accuracy was the same as that when no signal was given.

The fact that the subjects were able to report any row requested with high accuracy when they were queried immediately after the exposure indicates that they must have had an accurate memory of nearly all the items in the display. Apparently they were able to use a visual image which was virtually perfect at first but which persisted for less than 1 second. Other studies, based on other testing procedures, show that under these general conditions iconic memory persists for approximately 250 milliseconds [Haber and Standing, 1969]. These highly labile images probably act to provide continuity in our visual experiences—that is, to prolong the otherwise fleeting effects of visual stimulation. Thus iconic memory aids the integration of information in skills such as those involved in reading [Haber, 1970]. Iconic memory is not, of course, limited to vision. Comparable findings have been obtained in studies in which complex information is presented by means of tactile stimulation [Bliss et al., 1966].

Another type of imagelike memory, *eidetic imagery*, is found only in certain people, particularly children. In this case the subject reports that after looking at a visual display he retains a detailed image which may last for minutes, or sometimes longer, under some conditions. This image is not simply a visual *afterimage*, since it is lost if the subject attempts to move it to another surface. In contrast, a visual afterimage can be projected onto any neutral surface (note that a visual afterimage is also a type of memory). In one study of eidetic imagery Haber and Haber [1964] showed a series of pictures to elementary school children. As each picture was removed, the children were asked to keep looking at the area where the pictures had been displayed and to describe in detail all features of the image. Some of the subjects (approximately 8 percent) were able to examine the images and give extremely detailed reports. For example, one subject was shown a picture from *Alice in Wonderland* showing Alice looking up at the Cheshire Cat in a tree. After the picture was removed the subject was able to give an accurate description of it, including the number of stripes on the cat's tail. Interestingly, the availability of an eidetic image did not necessarily result in better memory of the picture after the image faded. When they were asked to describe the picture from "memory," the performance of children with eidetic imagery was no better, or only slightly better, than that of noneidetic children.

Little is known about eidetic imagery. In particular, we do not know why it occurs primarily in children. There is no evidence that eidetic images are normally used by such children as a form of memory, but any complete understanding of memory will have to consider the role of eidetic imagery as a special form of memory.

## SHORT-TERM AND LONG-TERM MEMORY

Most of us do not have eidetic imagery, and iconic memory is too labile to be the sole basis of our memory for recent events. Iconic memory may, however, be the first stage in a series of memory processes. Obviously we must have the capacity for "perfect memory," however brief, if we are to develop, with repetition, good retention over periods of time greater than 1 second. Memory lasting for several seconds or minutes after an experience is usually referred to as *short-term memory*. We have little difficulty remembering the last sentence we have heard or spoken. We can, with some effort, remember a telephone number long enough to dial it—that is, we can if it contains no more than seven digits (or if part of the number, such as the prefix or area code, is well learned in advance). Miller [1956] has pointed out that we are usually able to hold only seven (plus or minus two) items in short-term memory. If more items than this

**39**

are presented, accuracy generally does not improve unless the items are rehearsed or repeated.

We do not yet know what makes short-term memory "short term." There is some evidence that the rapid loss of retention following an experience may be due to a decay of the neurobiological trace of the experience. It is also clear, however, that short-term retention can be affected by interference from experiences that have occurred in the interval between the original experience and the retention test. This type of interference is termed *retroactive interference*. In one study Peterson and Peterson [1959] simply asked subjects to recall three letters at intervals ranging from 3 to 18 seconds after presentation. During the retention interval the subjects counted backward by threes or fours (to prevent rehearsal). As Fig. 2-2 shows, the percentage of letters recalled decreased directly with the retention interval. Only 10 percent correct recall was found after 18 seconds. Of course, this curve cannot be regarded as a "pure" short-term decay curve because of the possibility that the loss is caused by interference from the counting activity. We know that errors in dialing telephone numbers are increased simply by the requirement that a particular digit be dialed prior to the number [Conrad, 1958]. Apparently distraction of any kind can cause losses in short-term memory. Note, however, that similar distractions do not cause losses of retention of well-learned responses, such as your own telephone number.

Short-term memory is also affected by the acoustical *similarity* of the interfering information to material recently experienced [Broadbent, 1970]. Material which sounds like the original material is interfering. For example, if subjects are asked to remember the combination B C D and are then asked to copy the letters P T P V V T, the original letters are likely to be forgotten. However, copying the letters F L E M M L produces little interference [Wicklegren, 1965; Dale, 1964]. Also, in short-term memory similarity in meaning of the items does not appear to affect their recall. A sequence of words with similar meanings—broad, great, large, wide, big—is remembered as well as a sequence of words with different meanings—hot, old, strong, foul, deep [Baddeley, 1964]. Thus in short-term memory similarity of the sounds is much more important

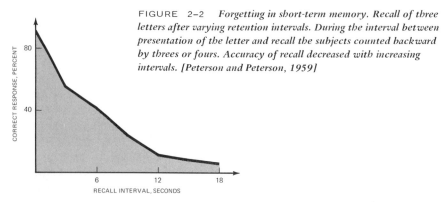

FIGURE 2-2    *Forgetting in short-term memory. Recall of three letters after varying retention intervals. During the interval between presentation of the letter and recall the subjects counted backward by threes or fours. Accuracy of recall decreased with increasing intervals. [Peterson and Peterson, 1959]*

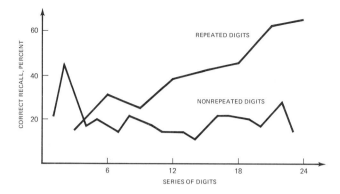

FIGURE 2–3 *Effect of repetition on recall of a series of 24 nine-digit numbers. Recall of each sequence was tested immediately after presentation. One nine-digit sequence was repeated in every third position in the series. Other points represent unrepeated nine-digit sequences. [Hebb, 1961]*

than similarity of the meaning. In contrast, similarity of meaning is very important in producing interference in long-term memory.

As we have just seen, we forget many of our experiences within a few seconds—and yet we know that experiences can leave fairly long-lasting memory. How do memories become permanent, or at least fairly long lasting? How is a recent experience stored in long-term memory? This question must be asked at two levels. We need to know the conditions which result in long-term memory, and ultimately we need to know the neurobiological (neuroanatomical, neurophysiological, and neurochemical) process underlying memory.

## THE ROLE OF REPETITION

Many factors influence the development of long-term memory. Perhaps the most important influence is repetition. Although practice does not necessarily "make perfect," it does lead to good retention, as we know from our own experiences as well as extensive experimental research. In a simple but elegant study Hebb [1961] studied the effect of repetition on memory for a series of digits. College students were read a series of nine digits at the rate of one per second and were instructed to repeat the digits in the same order. This task is called the *digit-span* test. Twenty-four series of numbers were presented. In 16 of them the sequence of the digits was varied randomly. However, every third sequence was a repetition of the same nine digits in the same order. Even though the subjects were not aware that one sequence was being repeated they benefited from the repetition. While performance on the randomized series of digits remained fairly stable over the tests, performance on the repeated series improved with repetition (see Fig. 2-3). These findings suggest that each experience produced short-term memory which provided a basis for partial recall of the random series (as in

**41**

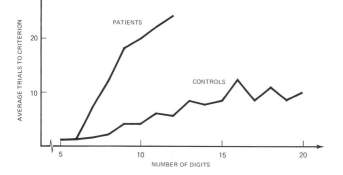

FIGURE 2–4   *Learning of series of digits by patients with temporal lobe brain damage and by college students. At all series larger than six digits the patients learned more slowly than did controls. For both groups the number of trials required to learn increased as the number of digits in the series was increased. [Drachman and Arbit, 1966]*

remembering a telephone number just looked up), as well as changes leading to the formation of more stable memory (as in *memorizing* a telephone number).

Under normal conditions repetition, through practice or rehearsal, is no doubt essential for memorizing, or "learning by heart." However, as we have seen, in some cases the capacity to memorize may be destroyed. Drachman and Arbit [1966] compared the performance of college students in digit-span learning tasks with that of patients with bilateral temporal lobe brain damage. All subjects were first given a digit-span test; the average scores of the two groups were not markedly different—seven digits for the patients and eight digits for the students. The subjects were then tested on successively longer series of digits, with each successive series repeated as necessary, up to 25 times. As Fig.  2-4 shows, for both groups the number of repetitions necessary for learning increased with the number of digits in the series. However, the patients were completely unable to learn a series of more than 11 digits, while the students were able to learn series as long as 20 digits after approximately 10 repetitions.

One of the subjects in this experiment was H.M., the patient discussed earlier in this chapter. H.M.'s digit span was six digits. He was completely unable to learn a series longer than this even with 24 repetitions. H.M. apparently lacked any capacity other than short-term memory for such material. This was also indicated by his performance on another memory task in which he was asked to say whether two stimuli, sounds and lights, presented in sequence were the same or different [Prisko, 1963]. Normal subjects are able to perform with no difficulty even if there is a 60-second interval between the two stimuli. H.M. made very few errors when less than 20 seconds elapsed between the two stimuli, but his performance was poor with a 60-second delay (see Fig.  2-5). On trials in which he was distracted during the interval his performance was no worse than on undistracted trials. Evidently his

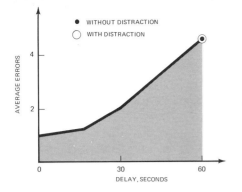

FIGURE 2–5    *Effect of temporal lobe surgery on short-term memory. Performance of the patient H.M. on a delayed-comparison memory task. The curve shows performance when the subject was distracted during the delay between the two stimuli to be compared. The open circle shows performance after a 60-second delay with no intervening distraction. [Prisco, 1963]*

short-term memory declined rapidly whether there was distraction or not.

Thus under certain abnormal conditions a person may have short-term memory but lack the ability to store experiences in a durable form. The Russian psychologist Luria [1968] has reported the extremely interesting case of the opposite difficulty. Apparently this person was unable to *avoid* storing his experiences, however trivial, in long-term memory. This "deficiency" caused interesting but unfortunate problems. Mr. S. was able to learn after only one presentation extremely complicated material, including numbers, nonsense passages, and passages in a foreign language. In one experiment he readily memorized a table of 52 digits (4 columns and 13 rows) within 3 minutes—a feat you might try yourself. He was able to report the numbers in any order requested, by columns, by rows, and even in diagonal zigzag patterns.

Not only was Mr. S. able to perform without error immediately after the material was presented, but he could also recall the material, still without error, when he was tested months later. This remarkable ability led him to become a professional memory expert, or "mnemonist." However, his major problem as a performer was that his memory was too perfect. He frequently gave several performances an evening, often in the same hall. In his recall of numbers written on a blackboard at one performance he had great difficulty ignoring his memory of the numbers written on the blackboard in earlier performances that evening or even previous evenings. He was plagued by an inability to forget. As Luria has asked [1968, p. 61]:

> How do we explain the tenacious hold these images had on his mind, his ability to retain them not only for years but for decades? . . . what explanation was there for the fact that . . . S could select at will any series ten, twelve, or even seventeen years after he had originally memorized it? How had he come by this capacity for indelible memory traces?

Mr. S.'s memory has been described, but it has not been explained. There is some indication that the ability may have been inherited; both of his parents and a nephew were also reported to have remarkable memory. However, we know nothing about the biological processes that would provide for such an ability. Clearly this "gift" is abnormal, and it is probably a good thing that we are not all afflicted with such talent. Mr. S.'s memory consisted of such detail that it limited his ability to function at an abstract level. The ability to forget is adaptive. The fact that normal memory is perfect, or near perfect, under two conditions – immediately after an experience and after repetition or rehearsal—makes it possible for us to remember best those events which are either recent or recurrent [Norman, 1969].

## MEMORY CONSOLIDATION

The cases of H.M. and Mr. S. are obviously extreme examples of disorders of memory functioning. In one case memory was too "perfect" and in the other the patient apparently had completely lost the ability to memorize—that is, to form long-term memory. Ordinarily, an experience produces both short-lasting and long-lasting memory. We do not yet know what changes take place in the nervous system when memories are stored, but it is clear that memory-storage processes can be greatly modified by alterations in neural functioning. It seems likely that an understanding of the nature of the neural alternations which affect memory may provide important clues to an eventual understanding of the neurobiological bases of memory storage.

It is well known that people who have suffered head injuries are often unable to remember the events immediately preceding the injury. This selective loss of memory for recent experiences is termed *retrograde amnesia*. Generally the degree of amnesia varies directly with the severity of the injury, but in some cases there is permanent loss of all memory of events which occurred minutes, hours, or even days prior to the accident [Russell and Nathan, 1946]. These clinical findings show that long-term memory is not immediately fixed, or consolidated, at the time of an experience. Rather, it appears that memory consolidation involves processes which are time dependent. Thus development of long-term memory can be prevented or seriously impaired by conditions which disrupt neural functioning.

The strongest evidence that the consolidation of long-term memory involves time-dependent memory-storage processes has come from laboratory studies of retrograde amnesia, especially studies of the effects of *electroconvulsive shock* (ECS) on memory. This technique consists in passing an electric current through the brain for a brief period of time. ECS treatment produces brain seizures. Thus it can be used to produce short-lasting but gross alterations in neural activity in experimental animals. Duncan [1949] found that rats were unable to learn a simple task if they were given an ECS treatment each day immediately after training. However, they learned normally if the treatment was given several hours after the training. The treatments caused the animals to forget the immediately preceding experiences; retrograde amnesia was produced in the laboratory. Similar findings have been obtained in numerous other experiments [Glickman, 1961; McGaugh, 1966; Jarvik, 1968].

In studies of ECS-induced retrograde amnesia animals are typically given a single training trial, an ECS treatment, and then a single retention test. In one common test, inhibitory avoidance learning, mice are given a mild foot shock as they step from one compartment of an apparatus to another. When they are retested at a later time (usually 24 hours or longer) animals that are otherwise untreated usually remain in the first compartment; they remember the foot shock. Animals given ECS treatment shortly after the training trial will readily reenter the second compartment when they are retested; they seem *not* to remember that they were punished. Degree of retention varies directly with the interval between the training and the ECS treatment; Fig. 2-6 shows a "gradient" of retrograde amnesia typically obtained in such experiments.

Numerous other techniques are highly effective in producing retrograde amnesia in the laboratory. Amnesic treatments include anesthetics, convulsant drugs, and antibiotics [Cherkin, 1969; Barondes, 1968; Agranoff, 1968]. Retrograde amnesia is not an all-or-none effect. The degree of amnesia produced by an amnesic treatment depends on such factors as the strain of animal used, the intensity of the electrical stimulation or drug dosage, and the duration of treatment. The effect also varies with the region of the brain that is treated. The entire brain can be affected by ECS or drug treatments, but retrograde amnesia can also be produced by delivering small amounts of electrical stimulation to specific regions of the brain [Wyers et al., 1968; Zornetzer and McGaugh, 1970] as well as by damage to specific regions of the brain [Hudspeth and Wilsoncroft, 1970]. With all treatments the effects are

FIGURE 2-6 *Typical gradient of retrograde amnesia obtained in experimental studies of memory disruption. Degree of retention increases as the interval between the training and the posttraining treatment is lengthened. The slope of the "gradient" varies with a number of conditions.*

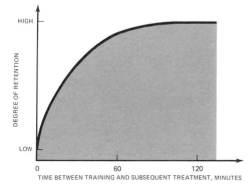

TIME BETWEEN TRAINING AND SUBSEQUENT TREATMENT, MINUTES

FIGURE 2-7 *Facilitation of learning with posttraining drug injections. Left, effects of different doses of pentylenetetrazol given daily immediately after training. Speed of learning varied directly with drug dose. Right, effects of time of drug injection (before or after daily training) on rate of learning. Marked facilitation of learning was found with injections given before training and up to 1 hour after training. Degree of facilitation decreased as the interval between training and drug injection was lengthened. [Krivanek and McGaugh, 1968; McGaugh and Krivanek, 1970]*

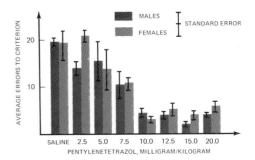

time dependent. Usually little or no effect is found if the treatments are administered several hours after training.

One interesting feature of experimentally induced retrograde amnesia is that it does not necessarily occur immediately after the amnesic treatment. Rather, it usually develops gradually over a period of hours or days. Geller and Jarvik [1968] found that mice given an ECS treatment after training remembered their training a few hours after the treatment but then gradually "forgot," or became amnesic, several hours later. This finding suggests that amnesic agents may act by directly interfering with the consolidation of long-term memory without destroying short-term memory processes [Barondes, 1968; Agranoff, 1968; McGaugh and Landfield, 1970].

The basis of this selective effect of amnesic agents on long-term memory is not yet understood. There is extensive evidence that retrograde amnesia can be produced by antibiotic drugs which interfere with the synthesis of protein, suggesting that protein synthesis may be involved in the consolidation of long-term memory. However, the amnesic effects of such drugs could also be due to some other general effect on neural functioning. The processes underlying long-term memory consolidation are highly labile, and it seems likely that consolidation can be impaired by any treatment which seriously disrupts neural functioning shortly after training. It may well be that interference with protein synthesis is the basis of amnesic effects, but a final conclusion must await further research.

Recent studies have shown that it is possible to *enhance* memory-storage processes with drugs or electrical stimulation administered shortly after training [McGaugh and Petrinovich, 1965]. That is, it is possible to produce *retrograde facilitation* of learning as well as retrograde amnesia. Most studies of drug facilitation of learning have employed drugs which stimulate the central nervous system. Krivanek and McGaugh [1968] gave mice different doses of the stimulant pentylenetetrazol each day immediately after brief training in a simple maze. Training was continued until each animal learned the maze. As Fig. 2-7 shows, the number of errors made in learning the maze was lowest in the groups given the highest drug doses. In another experiment McGaugh and

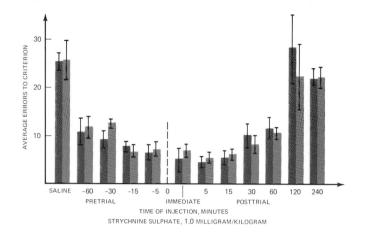

AVERAGE ERRORS TO CRITERION

SALINE  -60  -30  -15  -5  0  |  5  15  30  60  120  240
PRETRIAL        IMMEDIATE        POSTTRIAL
TIME OF INJECTION, MINUTES
STRYCHNINE SULPHATE, 1.0 MILLIGRAM/KILOGRAM

Krivanek [1970] injected different groups of mice with the stimulant strychnine sulfate at different intervals either before or after daily maze training. The best learning was exhibited by mice injected either shortly before or shortly after training, but learning facilitation occurred with injections given as long as 1 hour after training. Similar results have been obtained with electrical stimulation of brain structures.

The graded effect of retrograde facilitation suggests that these stimulants enhance learning by influencing time-dependent memory-storage processes in the central nervous system. An understanding of the action of drugs which facilitate learning may help provide an understanding of the neurobiological bases of memory storage. It seems likely that the facilitating effects of posttraining drug and electrical stimulation of the brain may have a common basis of action at the neural level. Much of the evidence from these studies indicates that the drugs act on brain structures which are involved in controlling arousal level. For example, Alpern [1968] found that the rate at which rats learned a discrimination maze was facilitated by implanting strychnine sulfate directly into the midbrain reticular formation which is located in the brain stem. Further, Denti et al. [1970] also found that learning was facilitated in rats by stimulation of the reticular formation with a small amount of electrical current each day immediately after training.

These studies of experimentally induced retrograde amnesia and retrograde facilitation of learning indicate that short-term memory and long-term memory are based on different processes, and that the processes of long-term memory remain labile for a fairly long time after training. We are only beginning to understand the nature of these time-dependent processes involved in memory storage.

The *consolidation hypothesis* of memory was originally proposed to explain the findings on learning and memory in humans. Mueller and Pilzecker [1900] reported that subjects forgot recently learned material if they were required to learn new material just after the original learning. Less forgetting resulted when a period of time elapsed between the two learning sessions. The second learning session was thought to interfere with the consolidation of neural processes initiated by the first session. Thus the hypothesis of consolidation was proposed as an explanation of *retroactive interference*—the interference with retention produced by new learning.

Although the consolidation hypothesis cannot account for all forms of retroactive interference it does appear that, for both short-term memory and long-term memory, retention is best when there is a minimum amount of interfering activity after learning. Tulving [1969] asked subjects to remember a list of 15 common words, which were presented one at a time, and instructed them to be certain to remember the word in the list that was the name of a famous person; they were to recall that name before proceeding to recall the other words in the list. The subjects were tested with different lists, with the name in a different position each time. They remembered the names with little difficulty. However, they had great difficulty remembering the word that came just before the name; recall of items presented just after the name was not impaired. Apparently the activities involved in learning and remembering the special word caused a mild retrograde amnesia. This type of retrograde amnesia may well account for a great deal of forgetting of insignificant daily experiences.

It is a common belief that retention is better if the material is studied just before bedtime. There is some experimental support of this observation. Several studies have shown that retention is better if the subject sleeps during the interval between learning and a retention test than it is if he remains awake during this time [Jenkins and Dallenbach, 1924; Van Ormer, 1932]. One interpretation of these findings is that the sleep period merely delays the beginning of retroactive interference. Another view is that sleep provides an opportunity for consolidation of the newly learned material and thus protects it from retroactive interference [Heine, 1914]. To examine the effects of sleep and activity on retention McGaugh taught verbal material to four groups of college students. Two of the groups learned at night just before going to sleep and the other two learned in the morning about an hour after awaking. One of each of these two groups then relearned the material 8 hours later and one other relearned 24 hours later. The two groups that went to sleep shortly after the learning period relearned the material much faster than the two groups that remained awake (Fig. 2-8). Even 16 hours of waking activity produced little forgetting if the subjects had slept for 8 hours following the original learning. Sleep appears to aid retention at least in part because it provides conditions favorable for consolidation of long-term memory. It may be, as suggested above, that sleep simply decreases interference occurring during consolidation of long-term memory. Another possibility is that neural processes that occur during sleep enhance consolidation. Several experiments have shown that if mice are deprived of rapid eye movement (REM) sleep, they tend to forget responses acquired just before the start of the deprivation period. Furthermore, retrograde amnesia can be produced by an ECS treatment given as long as two days after training if the animals are deprived of REM sleep during the interval between training and ECS treatment [Fishbein, 1970]. It is obvious that sleep has some influence on memory-storage processes, but we do not yet know why.

Since it is likely that memory-storage processes are active during sleep, is it possible to learn new material during sleep? Several investigators have reported some evidence of learning during sleep [Fox and Robbin, 1952], and on the basis of this evidence a number of manufacturers have marketed tape recorders for use in "sleep learning." Unfortunately, there is no real evidence that the subjects were actually asleep when the learning took place. As we know from our own experiences, we can be awakened for at least a short period of time by almost any abrupt change in stimulation—even *decreases* in stimulation. Weinberger and Lindsley [1964] found that cats were readily aroused from deep sleep (as measured by both behavior and EEG changes) by either an increase or a decrease in the intensity of a specific sound. You may have had the experience yourself of awakening when your clock stopped ticking.

It is evident that sleep does not cut us off from our sensory environment. If subjects are aroused from sleep when material is presented by an experimenter, then any learning that occurs may in fact occur while they are awake. To rule out this possibility Bruce et al. [1970] presented verbal material to subjects only when their EEG patterns showed a state of deep sleep. Under these conditions there was no evidence of learning during sleep. However, other research has shown that subjects can learn material presented while they are in deep sleep, as indicated by EEG patterns, if the presentation arouses them briefly. Koukkou and Lehmann [1968] read short sentences to subjects while they were in a sustained state of slow-wave sleep. The duration of wakefulness induced by the sentences was indicated by the length of time over which the EEG patterns changed from slow-wave sleep to a pattern found in waking states. The subjects were asked to recall the sentences when they were awakened 15 minutes to 2 hours later. Accuracy

FIGURE 2–8 *Effects of sleep and waking activity on retention. Retention as reported in savings scores was better in the two groups which learned just before going to sleep. When waking activity followed learning, the effect of 16 hours was no greater than that found with 8 hours. [McGaugh, unpublished findings]*

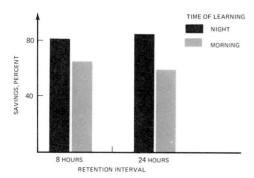

of recall varied directly with the length of the EEG wakefulness pattern elicited by the sentences. Of particular interest was the finding that they had no memory of sentences which elicited less than 30 seconds of wakefulness. Apparently material presented during sleep must cause at least 30 seconds of wakefulness if it is to be stored in long-term memory. Sleep machines may work, but if you plan to try one, be prepared to sacrifice your sleep.

## RECOGNITION, RECALL, AND RELEARNING

Memory is evidenced in a variety of familiar ways. Perhaps the simplest measure of memory is *recognition*. We are able to respond appropriately in our own complex environments because we are able to recognize the people, places, and things that we have recently or frequently experienced. "Objective tests," such as true-false and multiple-choice tests, are based on the assumption that the correct answer will be recognized on the basis of previous study of the material. We can indicate recognition merely by answering yes or no, but as we all know from our own guesses on such tests, the answer is not necessarily reliable evidence of memory. We can make "false positive" responses, which indicate recognition of events not previously experienced. We can also make "false negative" responses, which indicate failure to recognize events previously experienced.

Accuracy of recognition depends on the complexity of the information presented at the time of learning as well as at the time of testing. Under some conditions memory assessed by a recognition test is extremely accurate. For example, Haber and Standing [1969] showed subjects over 2000 pictures, at the rate of one every 10 seconds. An hour later the subjects were shown 280 pairs of pictures and were asked to select the member of each pair that they had previously seen. Somewhat surprisingly, 85 to 95 percent of their recognition responses were correct. This does not mean that they remembered every detail in every picture, but only that they remembered sufficient detail to distinguish pictures which were previously presented from those which were new.

*Recall* is a more complicated process, and it is subject to greater forgetting. This is one reason that many students prefer true-false tests over essay tests. You may not be able to recall the name of your second-grade teacher; you might immediately recognize it if you heard it. You may feel that the name is on the "tip of your tongue"—that is, you know, but are unable to recall. This experience is described by William James [1890, p. 251]:

Suppose we try to recall a forgotten name. The state of our consciousness is peculiar. There is a gap therein; but no mere gap. It is a gap that is intensively active. A sort of wraith of the name is in it, beckoning us in a given direction, making us at moments tingle with the sense of our closeness and then letting us sink back without the longed-for term. If wrong names are proposed to us, this singularly definite gap acts immediately so as to negate them. They do not fit into its mould. And the gap of one word does not feel like the gap of another, all empty content as both might seem necessarily to be when described as gaps.

Recent studies of "tip-of-the-tongue" memory have provided some understanding of the features of words which are important in recall. For example, the first and last letters of a word are more important than the middle letters [Brown and McNeill, 1966]. However, why is it that we are able to reject incorrect words without being able to recall the correct ones? As yet, we know little about the nature and bases of this phenomenon. Recall appears to require both retrieval and recognition; once a sought-for word is retrieved, we must be able to recognize it as the particular word which was sought.

Although recall can be highly accurate under some circumstances, it is also subject to a considerable degree of "creative" forgetting. Bartlett [1932] pointed out that a remembering experience is subject to many influences. New information is readily assimilated into knowledge that we have built up on the basis of our first experiences. In a real sense we filter much of our experience. Thus when we are asked to remember, we report our experiences as they have been modified by assimilation into our own schemata. Answers to essay questions are sometimes highly creative. In some instances information may be so distorted by organizing influences that subsequent recognition is difficult. For example, Hunter [1957] reported that he had once met a male student whose Nordic features so impressed him that he frequently thought of the young man later and visualized him as a Viking at the helm of a ship crossing the North Sea. When he encountered the student a month after this first meeting he did not recognize him and had to be introduced. The difficulty was that the student's appearance did not match the distorted recollection; his hair was darker, his eyes less blue, his build was less muscular, and he was wearing glasses. What we store and recall as memory depends on how we classify our experiences. Memory is not a passive process.

The relearning, or *savings*, method of studying retention was introduced by Ebbinghaus in his classical book *Memory* [1885]. The rationale is simple. We may retain some effects of prior learning of material even though we are unable to recognize or recall correctly. If we do have some degree of retention, then we should be able to relearn the material with less effort—fewer trials or less time—than would be required for original learning. That is, there should be some savings. The general formula used to calculate savings is

$$100 \times \frac{OL - RL}{OL}$$

where $OL$ is the measure of original learning and $RL$ is the measure of relearning. If no relearning is required—that is, if retention is perfect—the savings score will be 100 percent. If relearning requires the same effort as original learning, savings will be zero. Strictly speaking, the

**51**

savings method is used only when the material is learned to some specified criterion, such as one trial in which no errors are made. Thus its use
is restricted; however, it is an extremely sensitive technique for measuring retention. The findings reported in Fig. 2-8 were based on this
method of studying retention.

## ENVIRONMENT,
## BRAIN STATE, AND RETRIEVAL

As we have seen retention is measured in many ways. There is no "true"
measure of retention, and the evidence obtained depends on many conditions. It is well known that retention, by whatever measure, is best
when the conditions at the time of the retention test are similar to those
at the time of original learning. Examination grades for a course are
generally higher if the examination is given in the room where the lec-
tures were given. We often experience temporary difficulty remembering
the names of friends or colleagues when we are on vacation, that is, when
we are away from the environment where the names were learned and
used. Part of our difficulty in remembering childhood experiences may
be due to the absence of the environmental conditions under which the
learning occurred. In other words, in some cases it is the environment
that has changed, not the memory.

Reinstatement of the conditions under which the learning took
place can aid recall. For example, you may have forgotten how you
wrote when you were in the third grade, but you may be able to recall
and write that way again just by writing very slowly. Try this yourself:
write your name at the rate of approximately one letter each second or
two, and then compare the result with your regular signature and, if you
have a sample, your third-grade signature. There is some evidence that
recall is better under hypnosis [Reiff and Scheerer, 1959]. The effects
of hypnosis may be to reinstate some of the conditions, feelings, images,
etc., of the original learning situation. The phenomenal Mr. S. was able
to recall without error material he had learned years earlier, but before
doing so he first recalled very carefully the details of the situation, including the room, in which the learning had occurred.

The most striking demonstration of the importance of reinstatement of similar conditions in retention of learning was reported by Overton [1964]. Rats readily learned two conflicting responses, a left-turn
response and a right-turn response, in the same maze but under different
drug states. One response was taught while the rats were in a normal
state and the other was taught while they were heavily drugged with a
barbiturate. Overton found that their learning under one state was dissociated from their learning under the other state; the response that was
"recalled" depended completely on the rat's drug state at the time it
was tested. This is an extreme case of reinstatement, or state-dependency,
effects in retention, but it seems likely that much normal forgetting,
particularly temporary forgetting, may be due to differences in both

internal states and environmental conditions from those during learning.

A favorite scene in "B" movies and television is the one in which a captured suspect or spy, or perhaps a kidnapped heroine, is given an injection of "truth serum." This drug is supposed to make the captive reveal the secret formula, the plot, or an important incident. Drugs are sometimes used in psychiatric interviews and "voluntary" interrogation. Subjects interviewed under the influence of drugs such as sodium amytal are often quite communicative, but there is no evidence that they tell only the "truth." Drugged subjects may confess crimes they have never committed, and they may deny having committed crimes that they obviously have committed. The drug undoubtedly affects memory processes, but the subject is just as likely to report his fantasies as his "real" experiences [Freedman, 1960]. There is no pharmacological "pipeline" to truth.

Surgical procedures have also shed some light on memory consolidation. As mentioned earlier, severe epilepsy is often treated by surgical removal of a region of brain tissue which is the focus of the abnormal electrical activity and generates the epileptic seizures. In the course of surgery, which is done under local anesthetic, so that the patient remains conscious throughout the operation, the surgeon removes the skull overlying the brain and then stimulates the cortex with weak electric current. This is done in order to map the regions surrounding the epileptic focus and localize the region of the seizure, and so that regions involved in the control of speech will not be removed during the surgery (the patient's speech is blocked when the speech areas are stimulated by the current). Most of the seizure foci are found in the temporal lobes of the brain. This is the region which appears to be involved in memory consolidation in humans.

Several decades ago the great neurosurgeon Penfield reported that electrical stimulation of the exposed temporal cortex of human patients sometimes produced dramatic results [Penfield and Perot, 1963, p. 596]:

> A past experience, which had occurred regularly as a part of the patient's seizure pattern, was reproduced by electrical stimulation of the cortex of the temporal lobe. And also, more surprising still, a previous happening which was not related to previous attacks, was recalled by the surgeon's electrode.

The electrical stimulation appeared directly to elicit a vivid memory. Over the years experiential responses to mild electrical stimulation were reported by approximately 8 percent of over 500 patients whose temporal regions were explored. Such responses have never been elicited by stimulating any other regions of the brain cortex (see Fig. 2-9).

Many types of experiential responses have been obtained. Some are primarily auditory sounds and sound sequences such as conversations and music—and others are primarily visual scenes of persons or objects. Sometimes the experiences are complex ones with both visual and auditory aspects. The patient is fully aware that what he is experiencing is not based on real events occurring at the moment, but the experience

**53**

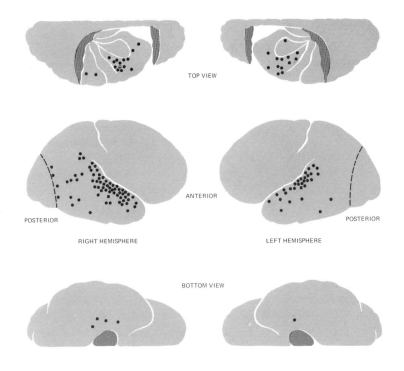

TOP VIEW

ANTERIOR

POSTERIOR

RIGHT HEMISPHERE

POSTERIOR

LEFT HEMISPHERE

BOTTOM VIEW

FIGURE 2–9 *Experiences produced by direct electrical stimulation of the brain in human patients. Dots indicate summary of all places in the two cerebral hemispheres where experimental responses were produced in patients. [Penfield and Perot, 1963]*

is more vivid than a recollection. For example, one patient responded in the following way to a series of stimulations applied to various regions of the temporal lobe [Penfield and Perot, 1963, pp. 640–641]:

During stimulation he said, "I am trying to find the name of a song." The electrode was removed. "There was a piano there and someone was playing. I could hear the song, you know. It is a song I have sung before but I cannot find out quite what the title of the song is. That was what I was trying to do when you finished stimulating!"

[The stimulation was then repeated without warning.] After removal of the electrode, he said, "Someone was speaking to another and he mentioned a name but I could not understand it." When asked whether he saw the person, he replied, "It was just like a *dream*." When asked if the person was there he said, "Yes, sir, about where the nurse with the eyeglasses is sitting over there."

[The stimulation was repeated] again without warning . . . and without questioning him. "Yes, 'Oh Marie, Oh Marie'—someone is singing it." He was then asked who it was and he replied, "I don't know, Doctor, I cannot recognize the voice."

[The stimulation was repeated] again without warning. He observed, while the electrode was being held in place, "Again, 'Oh Marie, Oh Marie.' " He explained that he had heard this before. "It is a theme song," he said, "on a radio program. The program is called the 'Life of Luigi.' " The patient then discussed the identity of the song with [the surgeon] and he ended by singing the well-known refrain, "Oh Marie, Oh Marie." All in the operating room recognized the song.

In some cases the experimental responses seemed clearly to be vivid memories of past experiences, while in others they seemed to be more like fantasies or hallucinations. As Penfield and Perot interpret these effects [1963, p. 679]:

The conclusion is inescapable that some, if not all, of these evoked responses represent activation of a neural mechanism that keeps the record of current experience. There is activation too of the emotional experience. The responses have that basic element of reference to the past that one associates with memory. But their vividness or wealth of detail and the sense of immediacy that goes with them serve to set them apart from the ordinary process of recollection which rarely displays such qualities.

By what process memory is evoked by brain stimulation remains one of the exciting and challenging problems for future research.

## FORGETTING OF LONG-TERM MEMORY

As we have seen, we forget for many reasons. The initial stages of memory, iconic and short-term memory, are highly labile. Forgetting can occur because of conditions which produce retrograde amnesia and interfere with consolidation of long-term memory. Forgetting can occur because of changes in external conditions and internal states which interfere with retrieval. In fact it almost seems that forgetting is the most salient phenomenon of memory. Even well-learned responses may be forgotten over time unless they are continually relearned or rehearsed. Although we usually do not think about it in this way, we maintain our skills, even our language skills, by constantly practicing them. At one point a colleague from a Spanish-speaking country spent several years in Italy, where he spoke only Italian. Upon his return to his native country he found he was unable to lecture in Spanish; his language was a strange combination of Italian and Spanish. Fortunately he completely recovered (relearned?) the ability to speak Spanish within a year following his return. Clearly he had forgotten.

What causes the forgetting of such well-learned responses? One possibility is that, with time, the neurobiological bases of memory decay or change, or that the memories simply fade. Another possibility is that two sets of well-learned responses compete with or obscure each other,

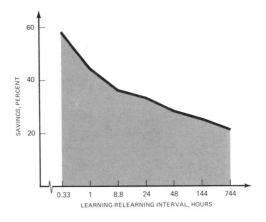

FIGURE 2–10   *Ebbinghaus' forgetting curve. Lists of nonsense syllables were learned at one period and relearned at one of several intervals. Curve shows percent savings score for each retention interval. Perfect retention would be 100 percent and complete forgetting would be 0 percent. Savings scores are computed as (original learning – relearning)/original learning. [Ebbinghaus, 1885]*

causing retroactive interference (if the later learning interferes with retention of earlier learning) or *proactive interference* (if older learning interferes with retention of more recently learned responses). Although these hypotheses are typically considered as alternative explanations, they need not be. In fact, forgetting of long-term memory may be caused by both interference and decay, as well as all the other influences mentioned. Ebbinghaus commented on forgetting as follows [1885, p. 62]:

All sorts of ideas, if left to themselves, are gradually forgotten. This fact is generally known. Groups or series of ideas which at first we could easily recollect or which recurred frequently of their own accord . . . gradually return more rarely, . . . and can be reproduced by voluntary effort only with difficulty and in part. After a longer period even this fails, except, to be sure, in rare instances.

Ebbinghaus conducted the first experimental studies of memory, and his approach, techniques, and findings provide a superb model of scientific investigation of a complex psychological problem. Over the course of several years he studied the effects of numerous conditions on learning and relearning of verbal material, using only himself as a subject. He developed the use of "nonsense syllables" and the savings method discussed above. He described many phenomena of memory, and for the most part, his conclusions have been substantiated by subsequent research. Among his major contributions was the first study of forgetting over time. In order to study forgetting, Ebbinghaus first learned eight series of lists, each consisting of 13 nonsense syllables. He then relearned one list at one of seven intervals—20 minutes, 1 hour, 9 hours, 2 days, 6 days, or 31 days—and repeated this complete procedure 163 times. Thus the measurements of learning and relearning were highly reliable. The forgetting curve obtained from these studies is shown in Fig. 2-10.

**56**

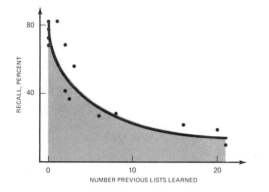

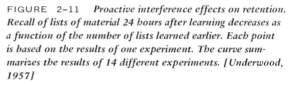

FIGURE 2-11  *Proactive interference effects on retention. Recall of lists of material 24 hours after learning decreases as a function of the number of lists learned earlier. Each point is based on the results of one experiment. The curve summarizes the results of 14 different experiments. [Underwood, 1957]*

As the figure shows, forgetting was rapid at first and then slowed; more forgetting occurred over the first 24 hours than between 24 hours and 31 days.

These findings and similar ones obtained from hundreds of other studies provide excellent descriptive evidence of forgetting over time. However, they do not explain why forgetting occurred. Some of it might be due to decay, but the procedures used also provided a great deal of both proactive and retroactive interference. Subsequent research has shown that in studies of this type forgetting over the first 24 hours depends largely on the number of lists that the subject has learned previously—that is, on proactive interference. Figure 2-11 summarizes a number of studies in which recall was measured 24 hours after learning. In spite of numerous differences in procedures, the results are surprisingly consistent. The degree of forgetting over a 24-hour period increases as a function of the number of lists previously learned. Subsequent research generally supports the view that a considerable amount of forgetting is due to interference, both retroactive and proactive. Learning does not always add to knowledge. It can make older memory difficult to retrieve, and it can interfere with both the learning and retention of subsequent information. The story is told that a university president who was an expert on fish set out to learn the names of all the students in the university; he gave up the effort when he discovered that he forgot the name of one fish for every student's name that he learned.

Is all forgetting over time caused by interference? In a series of experiments with rats Gleitman [1970] has found considerable evidence of forgetting which cannot be readily explained by interference or by changed stimulus conditions. He concludes that the interference hypothesis is attractive as an explanation of forgetting because it requires no

**57**

further physiological machinery beyond that required for learning, and it is equally possible that the underlying mechanism may be some decay process. We saw that there was rapid decay of short-term memory in the case of the patient H.M. It seems likely that long-term memory may also be subject to disintegration or decay with time. If so, the rate of disintegration should be subject to variations in biological states. Campbell [1967] has reported that weanling rats show much more forgetting over long intervals of time than adult rats. Gleitman [1970] has reported preliminary evidence that the rate of forgetting in goldfish varies with the temperature of the water in which the fish are kept during a retention interval of several weeks; forgetting was more rapid when the water was warm.

Deutsch [1969] has shown that in rats retention varies considerably with the amount of time between learning and testing. In one experiment Huppert and Deutsch [1969] trained rats in a Y-shaped discrimination maze. The rats were given 15 training trials in which they could escape from an electrified grid floor by entering the arm of the maze in which a light was on at the end of the alley. Rats in different groups were then given additional training to a criterion of 10 correct choices at one of 8 retention intervals. The best retention of the partially learned response was obtained in the groups trained either 7 or 10 days later. Performance at those times was clearly better than performance tested 30 minutes after the original learning. Furthermore retention was poor when the retraining occurred 17 days after the original training. In other words, retention first *improved* and then *declined* over time.

Deutsch has also shown that at the longer retention intervals, where considerable forgetting has occurred, memory can be improved by administering drugs which inhibit the enzyme acetylcholinesterase. This enzyme is responsible for hydrolyzing, or destroying, the molecules of the synaptic neurotransmitter acetylcholine. On the basis of this evidence he proposes that memory depends directly on the amount of acetylcholine available at synapses of the neurons which participate in the learning. The amount of acetylcholine is assumed first to increase with time after training and then to decrease. The rate of decrease is assumed to vary with the degree of original learning. Inhibiting the enzyme acetylcholinesterase with drugs should result in greater amounts of acetylcholine, and hence should improve memory if forgetting has occurred. This overall picture fits well with the hypothesis that changes in strength of memory with time are based on changes in neurotransmitter availability, but the evidence remains circumstantial. If this hypothesis is correct, the major question is what neurobiological processes underlie the alterations in transmitter levels? Nevertheless, Deutsch's findings do provide further evidence that changes in memory with time, including forgetting, are in part related to ongoing biological processes. There is reasonably clear evidence that memories do decay with time, even though we do not yet understand the biological processes which constitute decay.

As yet we do not know what neurobiological processes underlie memory. We do not know what changes in the nervous system must take place if experiences are to leave traces which affect subsequent behavior. If there is more than one type of memory trace, as

# NEUROBIOLOGICAL CORRELATES OF MEMORY

much of the evidence suggests, then the problem is enormously complicated. We need to know the neurobiological bases of each type of memory, as well as the possible interrelationships among the various memory processes. The questions of memory processes must be examined at several levels. We need to know how neurons are altered by experience and how different structures in the nervous system participate in the various aspects of memory processing. Finally, we need to relate these neurobiological findings to our understanding of memory gained from behavioral studies. A complete understanding of memory will require an integration of all levels.

Although we are quite far from an understanding of the neurobiological bases of memory, we are beginning to find neurobiological *correlates* of learning. That is, we are beginning to discover neurobiological changes which are associated with learning. The discovery of *correlates* is essential if *bases* are eventually to be understood. Our experiences produce a variety of anatomical, neurophysiological, and biochemical changes in our brains. Whether these changes are critical for memory storage or are merely byproducts of memory-storage processes remains to be seen.

## STRUCTURAL CORRELATES

The search for an anatomical locus of memory has been almost completely fruitless. Extensive studies by Lashley [1960] of the effects of lesions in various regions of rats' brains have turned up no evidence that retention of specific responses could be eliminated by selective destruction of specific brain areas. Brain lesions quite clearly interfere with learning and retention, as well as with other processes, but the neurobiological processes that underlie memory, termed *engrams* by Lashley, do not appear to be precisely located in discrete regions of the brain. If they are, the lesioning approach has as yet failed to find them.

A number of years ago it was discovered that the two cerebral hemispheres in man as well as other animals are functionally connected by the *cerebral commissures*, particularly the *corpus callosum*. When the commissures are cut by surgery, each hemisphere can function independently; the brain is split functionally as well as physically. In human patients commissural surgery is sometimes performed to alleviate severe epilepsy. Sperry [1968], who has conducted extensive studies of such split-brain patients, notes that each hemisphere has a "mind of its own," its own sensations, perceptions, ideas, memories, and experiences, all of which are unrelated to the corresponding experiences of the other hemisphere.

**59**

Although the patient can learn with either hemisphere, the two hemispheres learn quite different types of material. The dominant hemisphere, usually the left, is the only one capable of speaking and writing. Such patients are thus able to report in detail, talk about, only that information which reaches the left hemisphere. For example, split-brain patients cannot name or describe objects flashed in the left visual field because this visual information projects to the right (non-dominant) hemisphere of the brain. They are also unable to name objects held in the left hand because the sensory information from the left hand projects to the right hemisphere, which is unable to "talk." However, the right hemisphere functions better than the left hemisphere in memory for tactile experiences. In a study of short-term memory for tactile experiences split-brain patients were asked to grasp an unfamiliar and irregular wire form which was hidden from view and then select it by touch after a short delay from among several other forms. As Fig. 2-12 shows, they were almost completely unable to perform this simple task with their right hands (and left hemisphere). However, when they were tested with their left hands (their right hemispheres), most were able to respond correctly even after delays of longer than 2 minutes.

It appears that different regions of the human brain became specialized for processing and remembering different types of information. Thus memory processing is at least somewhat localized in the brain. It seems reasonable to anticipate additional evidence that different regions of the brain perform different functions in memory as we increase our knowledge of neuroanatomy and our ability to discover regions of the brain which are functionally connected.

If experiences produce changes in the neural processes which underlie memory, as we must certainly assume, then we should be able to observe the changes. The difficulty is that we are not yet sure what changes to look for, and it well may be that the critical changes are too

FIGURE 2–12   *Retention of a tactile experience in split-brain patients. Five of seven subjects were unable to perform correctly with the right hand. All could perform correctly with the left hand; four of the seven performed correctly even with a delay of 2 minutes. [Milner and Taylor, 1969]*

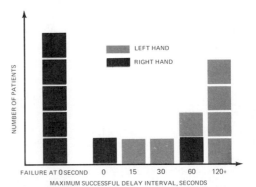

FIGURE 2–13    *Rats living in an enriched environment. "Toys" are changed frequently.* [*Rosenzweig, University of California, Berkeley*]

small to detect with current techniques. One possibility is that neural activity produced by training induces anatomical changes or growth in nerve cells and their processes. Evidence of alterations in the anatomy of neural tissue produced by specific training has eluded even the most imaginative researchers. However, as new techniques are developed for studying the fine structure of the nervous system, we may be able to detect more subtle differences than are presently discernible, and it is possible that these will indicate the effects of experience on brain anatomy.

We do know that gross alterations in brain tissue can be produced by experience. Bennett et al. [1964] compared the brains of rats reared in a complex environment with those of rats reared with restricted environmental stimulation (see Fig. 2-13) and found a number of important differences. The brain cortex tissue of the rats reared in the complex environment was heavier and thicker and activity of the enzyme acetylcholinesterase was higher than in rats deprived of such environmental stimulation. There was, of course, no difference in the number of neurons in the brain cortex; however, the increase in cortical thickness may have been due to an increase in number of glial cells. Other control experiments indicated that the effects were not due to differences in stress or amount of exercise. It seems likely that the neural changes are produced by the different sensory experiences of the animals. However, as these researchers have pointed out [Bennett et al., 1964, p. 619]:

> . . . finding these changes in the brain consequent upon experience does not demonstrate that they have anything to do with the storage of memory. The demonstration of such changes merely helps to establish the fact that the brain is responsive to environmental pressure—a fact demanded by physiological theories of learning and memory.

It is well known that the living brain generates electrical activity which can be readily measured and recorded. The dramatic technological advances in this method of investigation have led to numerous studies of the changes in electrophysiological responses during learning. In these "wire-tapping" procedures electrodes are temporarily or permanently implanted in the brain tissue, and the electrical activity is recorded from large regions of the brain, restricted structures, and even single cells.

Training has been found to produce changes in EEG patterns in different regions of the brain. Gross changes in brain wave patterns, such as desynchronization at the cortex and slow synchronous rhythms (theta waves) in the hippocampus, are commonly seen early in training but usually disappear with further training. John [1967] has found that under some conditions long-lasting changes in electrical activity can be produced by training. When an intermittent stimulus, such as a flashing light, is used as a signal for food for a hungry cat, rhythmic electrical activity of approximately the same frequency as the signal can be recorded from many structures in the animal's brain. These "labeled" responses may appear in different brain structures as training proceeds. If signals of different frequencies which have different consequences are used—say 10 hertz signals food and 6 hertz signals no food—the distributions of these labeled responses may become quite stable in various brain structures. Such changes are usually most marked in regions of the brain that are not involved in specific sensory processes. After animals are trained with such signals as flashing lights or particular frequencies, the responses can also be elicited by rhythmic electrical stimulation

FIGURE 2–14    *Average gross evoked responses to pattern of circles and squares. The evoked responses were recorded from human subjects stimulated by a weak flash which illuminated a visual field containing either a square or a circle. Each wave is based on 200 repetitions. The sequence of stimulation was large circle, large square, large circle, small square. Note the similarity of the evoked potential resulting from stimulation by large and small squares. [John, 1967]*

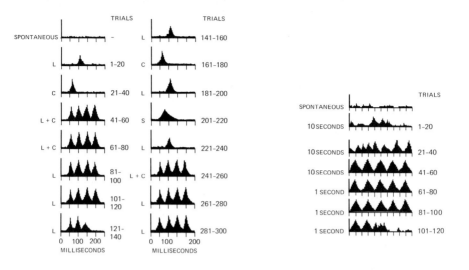

FIGURE 2–15 *Responses of single cells in a cat's visual cortex to various periods of sensory stimulation. Each line represents the distribution of responses summed over 20 stimulus presentations. At right, the response of a cell firing spontaneously followed by three series of 20 trials in which the cat was stimulated by a light flickering at 10 hertz. (The cell was in a region which was stimulated with anodal-surface positive current, but this is not a critical factor.) With the repeated stimulation the cell begins to respond at a rate of 10 hertz. It continues to respond at 10 hertz even when stimulation rate is changed to 1 hertz. The 10-hertz rate becomes weaker with repeated stimulation at 1 hertz. At left, the response of a cell (in another cat, not subjected to anodal cortical stimulation) following stimulation by a flash of light (L) and a click (C). When L and C are presented together, a new pattern of firing results. On trials 81 to 120 the L + C pattern is seen even though only L is presented. On trials 121 to 140 the response weakens, and by trials 141 to 200 the original L and C patterns return. The pattern of response to a shock (S) on trials 201 to 220 is different from the other patterns. After L and C are paired again on trials 241 to 260, L alone will elicit an L + C pattern. [Morrell, 1967, in John, 1967]*

applied directly to the regions of the brain from which the labeled responses were recorded.

In a very interesting series of experiments John demonstrated that the gross electrical responses of the brain evoked by sensory stimulation are modified by experience. In cats signals that have different consequences produce evoked potentials with different shapes [John, 1967]. Moreover, studies of evoked responses recorded from human subjects suggest that the wave shape of evoked potentials is related to the meaning of the stimulus. For example, brain response evoked by a square differs from that elicited by a circle (see Fig. 2-14).

Other studies have shown that the electrical responses of single neurons can be modified by experience. Morrell [1967] has recorded activity from single cells in the visual cortex of cats during stimulation with various patterns of lights and other stimuli. In one experiment anodal (positive) current was applied to the cat's cortex while the cat was stimulated with light flickering at the frequency of 10 hertz (see Fig. 2-15). After about 40 trials the cell began to respond at an average frequency of 10 bursts per second for about 50 trials. Morrell [1967]

**63**

also recorded the electrical activity of cells which were responsive to two or more types of sensory stimulation. Responses of one cell to a light and a click presented simultaneously were found to differ from responses to either stimulus presented alone. However, after presentation of the two stimuli together the same average pattern of firing was elicited by the light alone.

These findings indicate that patterns of neuronal activity can be markedly influenced by training. The EEG patterns appear to be correlates of learned responses. We do not yet know, however, whether they are *essential* components or merely *correlates* of memory-storage and retrieval processes.


## CHEMICAL CORRELATES

There is considerable interest in the possibility that memory might have a chemical basis. The spectacular success of recent research in molecular genetics has spawned numerous investigations of the effects of training on macromolecular synthesis in the brain. Research on this problem is a recent venture; speculation is not. In the last century William James anticipated this interest in molecular bases of memory [1890, p. 127]:

Every smallest stroke of virtue or of vice leaves its never so little scar. The drunken Rip Van Winkle, in Jefferson's play, excuses himself for every fresh dereliction by saying, "I won't count this time." Well! he may not count it; but it is being counted none the less. Down among his nerve-cells and fibres the molecules are counting it, registering and storing it up to be used against him when the next temptation comes.

Experiments with antibiotics which interfere with macromolecular synthesis suggest that memory storage may require protein synthesis. Since protein synthesis is directed by ribonucleic acid (RNA), it seems reasonable to expect that RNA might be affected by training. Several recent studies have shown that it is [Glassman, 1969]. For example, Zemp et al. [1966] found that training enhances RNA synthesis in mice. The effect was measured as an increased incorporation of radioactive ($H^3$) uridine in trained animals compared with stimulated but otherwise untrained animals injected with radioactive ($C^{14}$) uridine. The effect of training was seen in brain tissue, but not in liver or kidney tissue. However, the changes lasted for less than an hour. Thus they cannot be regarded as correlates of long-term memory. They may be due to processes involved in memory storage, or they may simply reflect processes involved in the maintenance or repair of stimulated cells. It is particularly interesting to note that the changes are most evident in the region of the hippocampus [Adair et al., 1968].

Changes in RNA associated with learning have been obtained in several types of studies. Hyden [1967] has shown that training may alter both the amount as well as the composition of neuronal and glial RNA. For example, Shashoua [1968] attached a small polystyrene float below the jaw of a goldfish. Within 3 to 4 hours the fish learned to adjust to this condition and swim fairly normally. Following the training the ratio of uracil to cytocine in the newly synthesized RNA was found to be markedly changed. In untrained fish the ratio was 3:1; in the trained fish it was 6:1. In several experiments with rats Hyden [1967] also found that various types of training produce changes in the base ratios of neuronal RNA. These findings also suggest that training alters protein, but it is not yet known whether such alterations are due to increased protein synthesis. Although there is substantial evidence that various kinds of experiences alter the synthesis of macromolecules, it is too early to conclude that such changes underlie memory consolidation. It would be important to know whether the time course of the development of these changes parallels the time course of consolidation measured in studies of retrograde amnesia produced by antibiotics.

Can memory be transferred from one individual to another? Is it possible to "transfer" memory by injecting an animal with an extract of the brain of another animal? This is probably the most dramatic, as well as controversial, question in current research on the neurobiological bases of memory. Evidence of "memory transfer" by such procedures would provide dramatic evidence that memory storage is based on chemical changes. Furthermore, the nature of the changes underlying memory could be discovered by determining the molecule responsible for the transfer. The hope of discovering "memory molecules" has stimulated a large number of memory-transfer experiments [Byrne, 1970]. The earliest experiments used planarians. Transfer was obtained by feeding trained planarians to naïve ones [McConnell, 1962]. Subsequent research has indicated, however, that equally effective transfer is obtained by feeding planarians other planarians that have been subjected to stimulation but are otherwise untrained [Hartry et al., 1964]. Thus the transfer effects do not appear to be due to transfer of any specific "memory molecule."

Most recent studies have used rats and mice [Golub et al., 1970]. The experiments have used a variety of behavioral and chemical procedures, as well as numerous criteria for "memory transfer." The findings have been extremely conflicting, and consequently it is impossible to draw any firm conclusions at this point. The bulk of the evidence indicates some sort of transfer effect, although no research has as yet been able to specify either optimal or reliable procedures for producing it. Moreover, it is not yet clear whether these effects, when they are obtained, are due to memory transfer or facilitation of learning [McGaugh, 1967]. The effects are most likely not due to RNA, but to some other molecule or molecules [Luttges et al., 1966; Ungar, 1970]. Should some of the experiments turn out to be reproducible, they may provide a clue to the molecular bases of memory storage. Such evidence would have interesting implications for education. Certainly the social, ethical, and scientific implications of "memory" transplants are even more far-reaching than those related to heart transplants. Nevertheless, we have not yet turned up a "memory molecule," and at least for the moment, you will have to continue to acquire information through the conventional neurobiological processes which underlie learning and memory. We have as yet developed no chemical substitute for study.

In this chapter we have briefly reviewed only an extremely limited selection of theories and research concerned with the nature and bases of memory. Obviously memory involves an incredibly complicated set of processes. When we are able to obtain a completely adequate understanding of memory processes, we shall be able to deal effectively with many of the disorders of memory, and perhaps even some types of mental retardation. The findings reported here indicate that progress is being made, but we will need to know a great deal more before we will understand the "machinery" of memory.

## SUMMARY

Memory represents the lasting effect of stimulation. The inability to remember or the inability to forget are thus severe handicaps in our ability to adapt to the environment. There appear to be several forms of memory processes. One type of imagelike memory, iconic memory, is represented by the fleeting images that provide continuity to our sensory experience. In another type of imagelike memory, eidetic imagery, detailed images can be remembered for many minutes or longer under appropriate conditions.

In addition to these special forms of memory, the processes of short-term memory appear to have different characteristics from those of long-term memory. Short-term memory, recollection for several seconds or minutes of details such as a sequence of digits, may be disrupted by either retroactive or proactive interference. These effects are influenced by such factors as acoustical similarity rather than meaning similarity of the interfering information.

The consolidation of short-term memory into long-term memory depends particularly on repetition or practice. Evidence that long-term memory involves time-dependent processes comes partly from studies of retrograde amnesia which can be produced experimentally by ECS or drug treatments. The degree of retrograde amnesia produced depends on the intensity of the treatment, the time between original learning and amnesic treatment, the type of animal, and other factors. It has also been possible to enhance memory with drug treatments or with electrical stimulation of certain parts of the brain. In addition, the consolidation hypothesis has received experimental support from studies of the effects of retroactive interference, and sleep on learning and memory.

Two measures of information retention and retrieval from memory are recognition and recall. The accuracy of recognition depends on such factors as the complexity of the information learned and the time of testing. Recall of long-term memory, which is subject to greater forgetting, has been used, for example, to study the phenomenon called tip-of-the-tongue memory. Recall is subject to a great deal of distortion, since memories are modified by information previously acquired. A limited but extremely sensitive measure of retention is provided by the amount of savings in relearning.

The psychobiological bases of memory processes represent an active area of research interest. Physiological and environmental states profoundly influence the ability of animals and men to recall previously learned information. Studies of forgetting indicate that the apparent loss of information from long-term storage may be influenced not only by interference, but by an intrinsic decay process. A number of neurobiological correlates of memory have been observed. Although the search for a precise anatomical locus of the engram has been fruitless, research with split-brain subjects points to areas of the brain, particularly the cerebral cortex, that play an important role in memory processes. Electrical activity of various areas of the brain has been shown to change with learning, as have such biochemical processes as RNA and protein synthesis in the brain.

**CHAPTER THREE**

## THINKING
## AND THE MIND

Thought and language are the most complex and important activities of man. They are the characteristics that set man apart from all other animals. Man is not the only animal that thinks. The higher mammals, particularly primates, think very well indeed; they can solve difficult problems and form very complex concepts. However, no species other than man has developed a genuine language. It is largely through the use of language that man has acquired culture and his knowledge of the world. Thought and language seem almost inextricably interwoven in man. Your ordinary thinking activity is invariably accompanied by the use of language, even if only to yourself. (Regrettably, the reverse is not always true.) In this chapter we will review thought and language, treating them as separate topics solely for convenience of discussion.

The study of human thinking is perhaps the most basic and also the most difficult area of psychology. Thought is largely a private activity. Your thoughts belong mostly to you and to no one else unless you choose to communicate them. Overt or behavioral signs of thinking are not easy to detect in normal adults, although young children, the men-

68

# THOUGHT
# AND LANGUAGE

tally retarded, and the mentally ill frequently do provide us with a running verbal and behavioral commentary on their thoughts—often in much greater detail than we might wish.

There is no specific or technical definition of thinking in psychology. Many aspects of thinking, particularly such problem-oriented behaviors as concept formation, problem solving, and creative thinking, which we term *directed thinking*, have been studied at length. However, thinking involves much more than simply working on problems. The common dictionary definition reflects what most of us mean by thinking: to have the mind occupied by some subject. It is very likely that we are always thinking when we are awake. You have no doubt had the experience of being asked what you were thinking about and replying "nothing," when a moment's reflection revealed that you actually had been thinking about something, usually something quite trivial.

This brings us to another undefined term—the *mind*. In fact thinking may really be said to be that which the mind does. Understanding the human mind is for many the fundamental goal of psychology. We cannot measure the mind's activity directly—only you know your own mind, and often even you do not know it very well—but we can study the behavioral expressions of this activity, the measurable indications

**69**

or signs of thought. In the seventeenth century the French mathematician René Descartes proposed a theory of the mind which has had enormous influence in psychology and philosophy and is still the view held by most laymen. The theory, which is very simple to describe but impossible to understand, retarded the development of psychology for at least 100 years and still causes great difficulties for many scientists. Descartes proposed that every human being has both a mind and a body, and that the body is material, made up of matter, but the mind is not. Furthermore, according to this theory, only men have minds; other animals are simply bodies or material machines. As flattering as this formulation may be to our sense of uniqueness, if mind is defined as nonmaterial, and not made up of the electrons, protons, and neutrons of matter—if it is not any conceivable "stuff," but some "nonstuff"—it would be impossible both in practice and in principle ever to measure, analyze, or study the mind by the methods and techniques of science. Thus, even if Descartes' theory is correct, we will never be able to study the mind scientifically. Consequently, the theory is either wrong or of no scientific value, since, by definition, it cannot be tested.

Rejection of Descartes' theory does not mean, of course, that we must also reject the concept of mind. Some psychologists have done this—most notably Watson, the founder of behaviorism, who championed the view that thinking consisted solely of small movements of the vocal apparatus, as when we talk to ourselves, and that this constituted the mind. Watson is claimed to have said, "I made up my windpipe this morning that there is no mind." Actually, the mind can be treated on the same basis as such concepts as learning, motivation, or intelligence. These are inferred phenomena, often termed *hypothetical constructs*. Just as we measure gravity, not directly, but in terms of its effect on objects, so we hypothesize or guess that a phenomenon or process occurs, describe its characteristics, and attempt to figure out ways that its operations will have some measurable effect that we can study. Thus learning is generally defined as an improvement in performance as a result of experience. We cannot measure learning directly—instead we measure performance, the responses of the organism. Learning is not a thing that you can hold in your hand. Gravity is perhaps a more familiar example. "Gravity" is a theoretical idea, a hypothetical construct—you cannot touch it or see it. However, from this theory physicists deduce certain measurable consequences—that objects exert gravitational forces on one another. If you doubt this, try jumping off the nearest building.

Mind, then, is no more mystical a concept than gravity. The major difference is that we think we know more about it from personal experience, whereas we actually know less about it in scientific terms. It is important to make a clear distinction between mind and conscious experience. Mind is a much more inclusive concept, referring to a wide variety of processes, both conscious and unconscious. The final arbiter of whether or not a construct or concept is of value is its utility or usefulness. Does it enable us to make meaningful and useful predictions about behavior? Of course. Our daily activities are determined in large part by our inferences about what is going on in other people's minds. We infer from their behavior that they have certain thoughts, ideas, and reasons in mind, and we predict correctly on this basis. If your girl friend is taking the pill, you have a rather good idea of what she has in mind. A good chess player correctly infers what is going on in the mind of his opponent. This is equally true, incidentally, when his opponent is a computer. There is a very famous answer to the question "can a computer think?" In a classical study of simulation of thinking, Turing [1950] proposed a game in which an interrogator, a man, and a computer were each placed in a separate room, with communication conducted by means of typed questions and answers. The interrogator could ask any question at all (except, of course, questions of the type "are you the computer?") and had to decide on the basis of the answers which was the computer and which was the man. Turing proved that in general it is not possible for the interrogator to distinguish. Such theoretically possible computers are often referred to as *Turing machines*.

The American legal system is another case in point. In many respects guilt or innocence depends on what occurred in the mind of a person who has committed a crime. Had he thought about it ahead of time (premeditation), and was he able to distinguish in his own mind between right and wrong (legal insanity)? This is not necessarily a proper interpretation of the construct "mind," only an illustration of its widespread use. In fact, in view of all that we know about the innumerable factors, many of them "unconscious," that determine behavior, the legal interpretation is, at the very least, inadequate.

In summary "mind" is a perfectly respectable scientific construct or hypothesis. Your own mind, particularly the part that forms your immediate stream of conscious experience, is largely your own private affair—but not entirely. The psychologist can determine with rather good accuracy some aspects of your individual mental activity. More generally mind is a legitimate subject of scientific study, and as we shall see, much is known about some aspects of the human mind and the minds of higher animals.

## NONDIRECTED THINKING

Psychology has emphasized the study of the directed aspects of thought—thinking about particular tasks such as the formation of concepts, the solving of problems, creative thinking, and discovery. This is, of course, only one part of thought. Idle thought, daydreaming and fantasy, conscious and unconscious processes, dreaming—these are the more general aspects of thinking and form the fabric of our everyday thinking activities. We think idly much of the time, particularly in ordinary conversation, and we solve problems only a small part of the time.

The terms "conscious" and "unconscious" seem to cause difficulties for some people, since like "mind," "learning," and "gravity" they are constructs that we cannot see or measure directly. Instead we rely on behavioral measures, the easiest and most reliable being verbal reports. A normal, cooperative adult can describe what it is that he is conscious of in considerable detail and with good reliability. The classic description of the stream of consciousness by William James is an example from a particularly intelligent and literate observer [James, 1890, p. 238]:

When Paul and Peter wake up in the same bed, and recognize that they have been asleep, each one of them mentally reaches back and makes connection with but *one* of the two streams of thought which were broken by the sleeping hours. As the current of an electrode buried in the ground unerringly finds its way to its own similarly buried mate, across no matter how much intervening earth; so Peter's present instantly finds out Peter's past, and never by mistake knits itself on to that of Paul. Paul's thought in turn is as little liable to go astray. The past thought of Peter is appropriated by the present Peter alone. He may have a *knowledge*, and a correct one too, of what Paul's last drowsy states of mind were as he sank into sleep, but it is an entirely different sort of knowledge from that which he has of his own last states. He *remembers* his own states, whilst he only *conceives* Paul's. Remembrance is like direct feeling; its object is suffused with a warmth and intimacy to which no object of mere conception ever attains. This quality of warmth and intimacy and immediacy is what Peter's *present* thought also possesses for itself. So sure as this present is me, is mine, it says, so sure is anything else that comes with the same warmth and intimacy and immediacy, me and mine. What the qualities called warmth and intimacy may in themselves be will have to be matter for future consideration. But whatever past feelings appear with those qualities must be admitted to receive the greeting of the present mental state, to be owned by it, and accepted as belonging together with it in a common self. This community of self is what the time-gap cannot break in twain, and is why a present thought, although not ignorant of the time-gap, can still regard itself as continuous with certain chosen portions of the past.

Consciousness, then, does not appear to itself chopped up in bits. Such words as "chain" or "train" do not describe it fitly as it presents itself in the first instance. It is nothing jointed; it flows. A "river" or a "stream" are the metaphors by which it is most naturally described. *In talking of it hereafter, let us call it the stream of thought, of consciousness, or of subjective life.*

Consciousness is measured as the sum total that you can describe about your own experience at any given point in time. What, then, is the *unconscious*? Very simply, it is everything else you might have been aware of, and hence might have said, but did not. More specifically, the unconscious is the totality of your past experience and current existence of which you are not aware at any particular time. There are many aspects to the unconscious, ranging from simple reflex phenomena, through memory, to complex unconscious motivation, all of which nevertheless have considerable bearing on many of our conscious activities.

Close your eyes and lift your arm part way. You can describe with considerable accuracy the position of your arm. There are several kinds of receptors that provide information to the brain about the position of a limb. In particular, pressure receptors in the joints signal the angle of bend of a limb, and stretch receptors in the muscles signal the degree of stretch of the various muscles involved. The activity of the sensory nerve fibers from both these sets of receptors provide adequate information about the position of the arm. We could, by recording the activity from either type of nerve fiber (the fibers differ in size), determine the position of your arm. However, only the joint receptors provide you with conscious information about the position of your arm. In experiments in which the joint receptors are temporarily blocked by a local anesthetic the subject cannot describe the position of his limb even though complete information is still provided to his central nervous system by the stretch receptors from the muscles. The subject is unconscious of this input. It plays a major role in the determination of limb position, particularly in relation to posture and such activities as walking and running, but it never enters into consciousness. There are many thousands of such reflex actions in the human organism, ranging from basic biochemical processes such as maintenance of proper acid-base balance to control of heart rate, blood pressure, and breathing, of which we are usually not conscious. This is a part of the unconscious.

The total amount of past experience and knowledge stored in the brain of a normal adult is almost inconceivable; it amounts to many billions of bits of information. Much of this information is available on demand. If, for example, you are asked for the numerical value of the mathematical constant pi, you immediately answer 3.14 (if you know, that is). The process involved in retrieving this information from among the billions of other bits of stored information was discussed in Chapter 12. The point here is simply that you were not conscious of "3.14" until you were asked. At any one point in time you are unconscious of most of your stored information and experience. This is another aspect of the unconscious.

These unconscious processes and knowledge are often referred to by psychoanalysts as the *preconscious*, to distinguish them from what is termed the *unconscious*. Freud developed a specific theory of the unconscious which is basically a theory of unconscious motivation. In simplified terms, a normal person is said to be unable to accept his own basic biological urgings or motivations, particularly those relating to sex and aggression, and relegates such matters to the unconscious, a murky and often evil territory of the mind filled with thoughts of sex and incest, rage, hatred, and the desire for death. Much of our behavior is said to be motivated and molded by unconscious forces. For some this view

**73**

has become reality rather than a theory; they make the unconscious a separate entity, much like Descartes' view of mind, but even less comprehensible.

More important than arguments over the merits of Freud's theory is the fact, established by Freud beyond question, that many aspects of human motivation are unconscious. A highly motivated person may be quite unable to tell you why he is so motivated. The case histories of clinical psychology and psychiatry are filled with examples illustrating the fact that people are quite commonly unaware and unable to describe the motives and reasons for their behavior, particularly when the behavior is abnormal or maladaptive.


## DAYDREAMING AND FANTASY

How many times were you told as a child to stop daydreaming and pay attention, or get to work, or whatever? Daydreaming is often considered an idle or wasteful activity. However, it is clear that everyone daydreams. Daydreaming means approximately the same thing as fantasy, although fantasy may be more extreme. All creative literature is really well-executed fantasy.

Studies by Singer [1966; 1968] have provided interesting information about daydreaming and fantasy. It appears that most people enjoy their daydreams and make active use of them both for pleasure and for problem solving. Content ranges from simple possibilities to wild dreams of inheriting a million dollars, being the Messiah, and obtaining a variety of normal and abnormal sexual satisfactions. Singer feels that nothing human (or inhuman) is alien to the imaginative realm of the accomplished daydreamer. Daydreams of men and women differ markedly in content, but not in frequency. Women tend to have daydreams involving passivity, a need for personal contact, and physical attractiveness, whereas the daydreams of men usually are much more concerned with explicit sexual activities. Singer categorized daydreaming as follows [1968, p. 2] :

*General* daydreaming reflected a predisposition to fantasy with great variety in content and often showed curiosity about other people rather than about the natural world.

*Self-recriminating* daydreaming was characterized by a high frequency of somewhat obsessional, verbally expressive but negatively-toned emotional reactions such as guilt and depression.

*Objective*, controlled, thoughtful daydreaming displayed a reflective, rather scientific and philosophically inclined content, and was associated with masculinity, emotional stability and curiosity about nature rather than about the human aspects of environment.

*Poorly controlled*, kaleidoscopic daydreaming reflected scattered thought and lack of systematic "story lines" in fantasy, as well as distractibility, boredom and self-abasement.

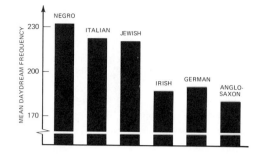

FIGURE 3-1 *Frequency of daydreaming for different groups in the New York area [Singer, 1968].*

*Autistic* daydreaming represented the breakthrough into consciousness of material associated with nocturnal dreaming. It reflected the kind of dreamy, poorly controlled quality of inner experience often reported clinically by schizoid individuals.

*Neurotic*, self-conscious daydreaming revealed one of the clearest patterns—the one most closely associated with measures of neuroticism and emotional instability. It involved repetitive, egocentric and body-centered fantasies.

The frequency of daydreaming appears related to relative social insecurity, at least in studies by Singer in the New York area. As indicated in Fig. 3-1, persons from Negro, Italian, or Jewish subcultures had much higher frequencies of daydreaming than those from Irish, German, and Anglo-Saxon subcultures. The content differed considerably for each group. The Irish showed a tendency toward religious, extremely fantastic, or heroic daydreams, while Negroes fantasized about sensual satisfactions, eating well, comfort, fine clothes, and cars. This would seem to fit rather well into a general view that unmet needs or motives, both biological and social, form the basis of much of our daydreaming. At a very simple level, you have probably noticed that when you are thirsty your own idle thoughts tend toward something cold to drink and when you are sexually frustrated your thoughts tend toward something not so cold.

Dreaming while asleep, which was discussed at length in Chapter 10, is a rather different and often far more vivid and compelling kind of fantasy than daydreaming.

## DISORDERED OR AUTISTIC THINKING

Autistic thinking refers to the abnormal or disordered thought that is characteristic of schizophrenia. The thought processes of schizophrenics, particularly in idle thought and daydreaming, are markedly different from those of most people. The idle thoughts of normal people have a certain degree of logic or coherency. For example, if you ask a person what he would do with a million dollars, he will think about ways to

**75**

THOUGHT AND LANGUAGE

spend it, invest it, or give it away. A schizophrenic might respond, "I have a million dollars and there are six white horses and the voice said I must . . ." White [1926] has recorded a characteristic example of autistic thought [in Morgan and Lovell, 1948, pp. 538–539]:

One patient was asked: "What did you say the other night to the students?" He replied: "Told them about locks and keys." "What else?" "Myriads of us keep growing in numbers, also in largeness; locks and keys, keys, keys, locks, locks, keys, keys, locks, locks, keys, keys, locks. Myriads of us quick-foot through, ev-er no mat-ter. Locks, keys, keys, locks, locks, keys, keys. Myriads of us ev-er full us as keep lives giant's growths, ev-er lives giant's keeper, ev-er no mat-ter. Locks, keys, keys, locks, locks, keys, keys, locks. Lives giant's wealth, health and pleasures, ev-er no mat-ter."

## DIRECTED THINKING

Higher organisms, certainly from the level of the rat up to man, give behavioral signs of directed thinking. In a very general sense directed thought is thought related to the external environment—adequate responses to stimulation, solving problems, forming concepts, making discoveries. Hebb [1949] gave a good behavioral definition of directed thinking as "some sort of process that is not fully controlled by environmental stimulation yet cooperates closely with that stimulation . . . the [observance of a] delay between stimulation and response."

In addition to a delay, directed thinking entails transformations between stimulus input and response. A simple example is *clustering* of items in recall. Try the following experiment. Select four common names from each of four categories—four planets, four fruits, four animals, four first names—write each on a separate card, shuffle them into a random sequence, and have someone go through the 16 cards once. Then ask him to recall the 16 words. He will recall them, not in the order you presented, but by category. You might object that this is merely a simple learning task and does not involve thought. However, the occurrence of clustering reveals the transformational aspect of directed thought. Thought and learning are, of course, closely interrelated. The distinction between classical learning, as in Pavlov's conditioned reflex, and thinking, as in Einstein's development of the theory of relativity, may in part be a matter of degree. Learning is involved in both activities, but Einstein's efforts included considerably more thought. Between these extremes there is a wide range of behavior that entails some degree of directed thought.

In a classical experiment Hunter [1913] showed that animals as lowly as the rat could learn a *delayed reaction*. As indicated in Fig. 3-2,

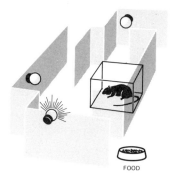

FIGURE 3-2    *Delayed-reaction experiment. One of the three lights goes on, indicating correct location of food, and then goes off. The animal is required to wait for varying periods of time after the light goes off before being released to go for the food.*

FOOD

FIGURE 3-3    *The* umweg *(roundabout) problem. The animal must go away from the food in order to go around the barrier and obtain the food.*

FOOD

the rat was placed in a start box from where it could see three light bulbs, one of which was lit and baited with food. After the light was turned off, the rat was kept in the start box for a period of time and then released. It had to "remember," or "keep symbolically in mind," which of the lights was on. In Hunter's original experiment rats could do this for 10 seconds, cats for 18 seconds, dogs for 3 minutes, a two-and-a-half-year-old child for 50 seconds, and a five-year-old child for at least 20 minutes. Actually the amount of delay time an animal can handle varies markedly with the particular conditions, but even rats can locate the right bulb after some delay. This might, of course, be termed only short-term memory. Nevertheless, it fits within Hebb's general definition of directed thought.

A somewhat more difficult problem is the *umweg* (roundabout) situation (see Fig. 3-3), in which the animal can see the food through the wire screen but must head away from it in order to reach it. Dogs can solve this problem, but rats cannot. At a still more complex level, if a food object is held above reach and a box is lying nearby, a chimpanzee will push the box over to the food, climb up, and get the food. A dog, although physically capable of doing this, will not. Such examples will be accepted by most people as evidence of simple thinking. We seem to be describing a kind of evolutionary or phylogenetic species-comparative intelligence test. This is not necessarily the case. It is difficult to find a task on which animal intelligence or ability to think can be compared directly across species. For example, the chimp uses the box in part because he is a climbing animal; the dog is not. Apart from the problem of comparison across species, however, there is ample evidence of simple directed thinking in nonhuman animals.

What do the terms in each of the following pairs have in common?

apple—orange
wheel—donut
fly—tree
Platonic ideal—categorical imperative
wood—song

The apple and the orange, of course, are both fruits. The wheel and the donut are both round. About the only thing "fly" and "tree" have in common is that they are both living things. "Categorical imperative" and "Platonic ideal" are both philosophical concepts of idealism (or both meaningless terms, depending on your point of view), "wood" and "song" do not seem to have anything in common, except that each has four letters. These are simple examples of concepts. A *concept* is a somewhat general category or term that includes several objects or terms within it. It is generally agreed in psychology that an organism has a *concept* if it has a disposition on the basis of which it can make nominal classificatory statements or responses ("this is X, that is not X") [Van de Greer and Jaspars, 1966]. This is a somewhat elaborate way of saying that concepts are categories of things or terms. Concepts are not correct or incorrect, or mutually exclusive. "Apple" and "orange" are both fruits; they are also both plants, both round, both sweet, and so on. Concepts need not have any reference to the real world—witness the two philosophical formulations.

Concepts can be developed by lower animals as well as man. Language is often involved in concept learning in man, but it does not appear to be essential. Hebb [1958] made the important observation that if different organisms are trained in the same kind of visual form discrimination, they may learn quite different things. For example, rats, chimpanzees, and two-year-old children were trained to choose a triangle form (1 in Fig. 3-4). The chimps took longer to learn this simple task than the rats. When the rats were tested with other triangle forms (2, 3, and 4), they had to start all over again; they had not formed a general concept of "triangle." However, the chimps did in fact form a

FIGURE 3-4    *Degree of concept learning of triangularity. Trained to respond to figure 1, the rat makes random re sponses to diagrams 2, 3, and 4; chimpanzees respond correctly to 2 and 3; and two-year-old human children re- spond correctly to 2, 3, and 4. [Hebb, 1958]*

THOUGHT AND LANGUAGE

somewhat general concept. They responded to forms 2 and 3, even though their initial training was to only one specific triangle. The children did even better, responding to forms 2, 3, and 4. This seems to be characteristic of children after infancy; they tend to *generalize* from one instance to another. It is almost as if the forming and use of concepts were a natural part of primate behavior.

It has often been noted that concept development seems to occur suddenly as *insight*, often referred to as the "aha" phenomenon. In his classical study of apes on Tenerife Island Köhler [1925] described a chimpanzee faced with the problem of retrieving a banana lying outside his cage. He had two sticks, one of which could fit inside the other, but neither of which was long enough to reach the banana. He tried for a while to reach the banana with each stick and gave up. Later, while he was playing with the sticks, he accidentally discovered they could be put together. He immediately did this, rushed to the edge of the cage, and pulled in the banana. Gestalt psychologists hold that such insights entail a spontaneous reordering of the organism's conceptual world—that they occur suddenly and *de novo*. In further studies on the chimp's use of sticks to obtain food Birch [1945] found that the more prior experience he had with the stick, the more easily he formed the concept of using the stick to obtain food. It seemed that once the chimp had learned to use the stick as an extension of his arm reach, he was able to generalize this use to a variety of situations. Birch concluded that the ability to reorganize previous experiences in accordance with the requirements of a new problem situation is the essence of problem solving.

Spence [1938], a reinforcement theorist and student of Clark Hull, held that learning, even learning of concepts, is the result of trial-and-error performance that is appropriately rewarded and punished. His analysis of the learning curves of chimpanzees on discrimination-learning tasks revealed that "sudden" learning with particular stimuli was closely correlated with the number of previous rewards and frustrations an animal had experienced with these stimuli. Spence concluded that the results failed to support the interpretation that sudden solutions are marked by the presence of insight independent of past reinforcement history.

Bertrand Russell once suggested that apes in American psychology laboratories form concepts by running blindly about using only trial-and-error methods, whereas apes in German laboratories sit quietly and evolve concepts out of their inner consciousness. The truth seems to be somewhere in between. Wisconsin monkeys utilize trial-and-error learning, but they learn more than the solutions to particular problems. As we saw in **Chapter 4**, they form *learning sets*—that is, they learn how to learn. In a comparison of learning-set performance by rhesus monkeys and human three- to five-year-old children on sets of discrimination-reversal problems it is clear that the children win. However, note that the discrimination-reversal data in Fig. **3-5** clearly illustrate set-formation and transfer-producing adaptable abilities, rather than specific bonds.

**79**

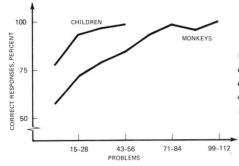

FIGURE 3-5    *Learning-set performance of rhesus monkeys and young children on discrimination reversal problems. The curves are based on trial 2 responses. [Harlow, 1949a]*

Without the monkey's learning curves we might be tempted to assume that the children's better performance indicates a gulf between human and subhuman learning. However, the extremely rapid learning by the children is not unlike the rapid learning by the monkeys, and an analysis of the error-producing factors shows that the same basic mechanisms are operating in both cases.

Reinforcement theorists such as Hull and Spence have constantly emphasized the need for a historical approach to learning, but their actual research on the influence of experience has been largely limited to the development of isolated habits and their generalization. Hence their failure to find any discontinuity in learning may stem from their study of individual rather than repetitive learning situations. Gestalt theorists (e.g., Köhler), unlike reinforcement theorists, have stressed insight and hypothesis in their description of learning, giving the impression that these phenomena are properties of the innate organization of the individual. However, if such phenomena do appear independently of a gradual learning history, they have not been found in the primate order.

There have been numerous studies of concept development in humans. The standard experimental situation employs objects that vary in form, color, and size (see **Fig. 3-6**). The concept the subject is to learn may consist of any one or more of these three dimensions. For example, suppose "blue square" is the concept; all the stimulus patterns which embody both blueness and squareness (there are three in the figure) are positive instances, and all which do not—24 in all—are negative instances. In an experiment the subject might be given each stimulus separately and instructed to guess whether or not it is "correct." He would then be told whether he was right or wrong.

Early studies by Hull and others investigated the relative difficulty of simple concepts. Heidbreder [1946], for example, had subjects learn nonsense terms for particular concepts; examples are shown in **Fig. 3-7**. The subject would then be tested on the next trial with a different picture of the same thing. The results of these studies indicated that simple concrete object concepts, such as face, building, or tree, were the easiest to learn, followed by spatial form and color, and then number.

In a careful analysis of conceptual behavior Bourne [1966] has distinguished between *stimulus attributes* and *conceptual rules*. The stimulus attributes are such things as shape, color, and size, each with numerous gradations, and the conceptual rules are rules for grouping stimuli on the basis of their attributes—that is, the rules are the general form of the concept. Bourne uses as a simplified example the development of the learning set for oddity in monkeys (Fig. 3-8). In this task the monkey is presented with a set of three stimulus objects, one of which is different from the other two. He is allowed to choose one of the objects. If he chooses the odd one—in this case the triangle—he is rewarded with food, candy, or some other incentive. If he chooses incorrectly, all the objects are removed and no reward is given. On the second trial the same objects are presented, but in different positions, and the monkey is again allowed to choose and is rewarded for a correct choice.

After several trials with these three objects three new objects are presented, with the oddity based on a different stimulus attribute—for example, this time one block may be larger than the other two. Once again, the odd object is associated with reward. This procedure is continued over a series of problems, each with different stimulus

FIGURE 3-6    *A set of geometric designs illustrating the kinds of stimuli and dimensions (shape, size, and color) used in many human concept-learning experiments [Moon and Harlow in Bourne, 1966].*

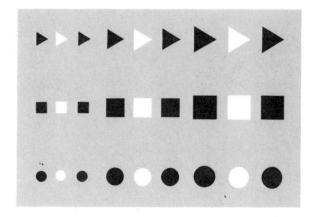

FIGURE 3-7    *Examples of stimuli and nonsense concept "words" used in studies comparing the difficulty of learning simple concepts in man [Heidbreder, 1946].*

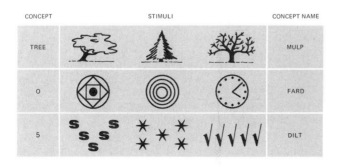

| CONCEPT | STIMULI | | | CONCEPT NAME |
|---------|---------|--|--|--------------|
| TREE | | | | MULP |
| O | | | | FARD |
| 5 | | | | DILT |

FIGURE 3-8    *The oddity principle. Left, a monkey solving an oddity problem [Harlow, University of Wisconsin]. Below, three sample oddity problems. The subject is rewarded on each trial only if he chooses or responds to the odd member (marked +) of each stimulus set. The first graph shows performance changes over trials within single oddity problems. The learning function is elevated with successive problems until, after very many problems, performance is errorless. The second graph shows actual data from a study of oddity learning in monkeys [Moon and Harlow, 1955]. The score plotted on the ordinate is the percentage of responses to the odd stimulus on trial 1 of each problem. After 250 problems these subjects make about 90 percent correct trial 1 responses. [Bourne, 1966]*

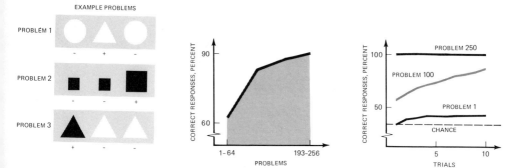

objects and a different cue or critical attribute, but the rule is always the same—reward is associated with the odd object of the group. Subjects improve both within problems (particular stimulus-attribute learning) and across problems (learning set). After a good deal of training the subject nearly always scores perfectly on new oddity problems. He has learned the concept of oddity. As Bourne notes, the oddity rule is a simple one, perhaps too obvious for most adults to appreciate fully. However, the data indicate that oddity is not a simple concept for a young or naïve subject; it is acquired only through extensive practice. Oddity, then, is a simple example of a general rule that is independent of particular stimulus qualities and refers only to the abstraction "same or different."

Bruner et al. [1956] introduced three types of rules in concept learning, conjunctive, disjunctive, and relational. A conjunctive rule requires that two stimulus attributes be present, such as red and square. A disjunctive rule requires that either one stimulus attribute or the other be present, such as red *or* square. A relational rule requires a comparison; in a simplified situation when two objects are compared each time, the larger of each pair is correct, independent of absolute attributes. In general it appears that disjunctive concepts are the most difficult to learn. An additional important finding was that people typically adopt certain kinds of strategies in trying to attain concepts. One example is *successive scanning*. The subject adopts a hypothesis, tries it until it is proved wrong, then adopts another, and so on, always attempting to remember and not reuse previous incorrect hypotheses. Another example is the more risky strategy of *focus gambling*, in which the sub-

82

ject changes more than one stimulus attribute at a time in an attempt to hit on the correct combination of attributes for the concept.

Still another formulation of the general features of concept strategy is the TOTE system of Miller et al. [1960]. Having formed a hypothesis, the subject *tests* (T) it against new problems or data. If it proves wrong, an *operate* (O) phase is instituted that generates a new hypothesis. This continues until *tests* (T) against new problems do not contradict the hypothesis, at which point the subject *exits* (E) from the problem situation. These strategy formulations are not restricted, of course, to particular experimental problems, but also apply to human behavior in complex real-life problem situations.

## PROBLEM SOLVING

Concept formation and problem solving overlap considerably; both are types of problem situations. They are sometimes distinguished in terms of the "correctness" of a solution. A specific problem may have only one solution, but a concept solution can have several correct forms—for example, an apple and an orange are both fruit and are also both round. This difference is also reflected in the distinction between *inductive* and *deductive* logic. Inductive logic is the formulation of a general law or principle to explain or apply to many specific examples. A common use of inductive logic is in science—the general theories and laws of science are inductions or concepts. Inductive logic is the forming of concepts. In simple terms it consists of making educated guesses about the world.

In deductive logic, on the other hand, we are given a set of terms and a set of rules and asked to prove or disprove a particular hypothesis. Geometry is a familiar example. To prove the Pythagorean theorem which says that the sum of the squares of the two sides of a right triangle equals the square of the hypotenuse you must use the rules and terms of Euclidean geometry in a fixed and prescribed way. Indeed, all of formal mathematics is deductive logic—it can be deduced from basic rules of logic. In actual fact, it is unlikely that human beings solve deductive problems in a purely deductive manner. As we noted above, subjects quite typically adopt and test hypotheses in trying to solve problems. This is inductive rather than deductive thinking. A particularly clear example is provided by the famous Indian mathematician Srinivase Ramanujan. He had no formal education beyond high school, and yet, almost entirely on his own and with little knowledge of past work in mathematics, he discovered more than 6000 theorems in mathematics, some previously known and many quite new. He did not develop and prove the theorems deductively, but worked almost entirely by "intuition"—inductive thought. Subsequent efforts proved him correct in most instances. Newman [1956] has described Ramanujan's work as the "most prodigious feat ever accomplished in the history of thought." His thinking was almost purely inductive in mathematics, an area that is in formal terms a purely deductive field.

**83**

You have had considerable experience in solving problems and are quite familiar with the general features of problem-solving behavior. If you wish to do an observational study yourself, try working out the correct solution to the "missionaries and cannibals" problem and note down each step, both correct and incorrect, that you make:

Three missionaries and three cannibals wish to cross a river. All can row, but their boat will carry only two people. It must never happen that on any shore there are more cannibals than missionaries, for the missionaries would promptly be eaten. The task is to specify the schedule of boat loads back and forth across the river so that all six will eventually end up safely on the far side of the river.

An actual solution process for this problem is shown in **Fig. 3-9**. The subject's initial behavior consisted largely in trying out various alternatives, first more or less mechanically on a trial-and-error basis—the first six steps. As many of these proved incorrect, he tended to develop hypotheses, and finally developed a new concept—staying in the boat—which ultimately led to the correct solution of the problem.

Specific problem tasks such as this can be solved by computers as well as or better than by men. An excellent example of this is the General Problem Solver (GPS) computer program developed by Newell and Simon [1963]. They set the program to derive the theorems in *Principia Mathematica*, the classic work by Bertrand Russell and Alfred North Whitehead, in which all mathematics is deduced from the rules of logic.

FIGURE 3-9    *A typical solution to the missionaries and cannibals problem. The green square stands for missionary and the blue circle stands for cannibal. Locations of the six men and the boat are indicated before each step. A cross marks the spot where a missionary passed on to greater rewards. [after Newell, 1968]*

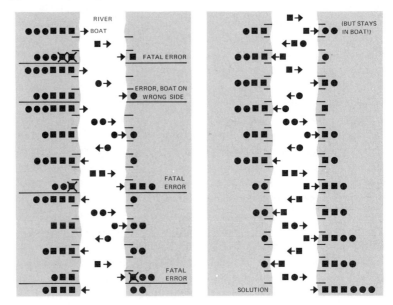

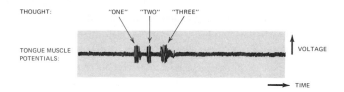

FIGURE 3-10    *Muscle potentials (voltage measurement) generated by the tongue as a subject thinks of counting "one," "two," "three" [after Jacobson, 1931].*

In at least one instance the computer produced a shorter proof than had Russell and Whitehead. According to the story, the proof was sent to Russell and he wired back congratulating the computer on developing a more elegant proof.

The GPS was intended to do more than high-powered logical deduction; it was an attempt to program a computer to solve problems in the same general way that people do. The program has been remarkably successful in this respect and does in fact solve many problems of the missionaries-and-cannibals type in much the same way that people do. The issue is the extent to which such programs can tell us more about how people actually think. One might suppose that there would be an endless variety of such programs. Actually, so far there are only a few general types of programs possible that will solve problems in this way. Perhaps as this approach is developed further the computer may be able to tell us much about the general features of human thinking, at least at the problem-solving level.

## THE NEURAL BASIS OF THOUGHT

Most of us take for granted that thinking occurs in the brain. However, some brave theorists have asserted that thinking is an entirely peripheral activity done with the muscles and involving the central nervous system only in so far as the formation of learned connections is concerned. Watson, as we noted earlier, was perhaps the first to propose such a theory. More recently Skinner [1957] developed a somewhat similar view. In essence small movements of the vocal apparatus—tongue, lips, throat, and chest—are assumed to occur whenever we think. These movements, the behavioral representation of nonspoken words, are chained together through reinforcement learning. It is quite possible to represent human thought with sufficiently complex interchaining of sequences of such movements.

Early experiments in which the muscle activity of the tongue and throat were recorded electrically during thinking gave considerable support to such a view. An example from the pioneering work of Jacobson [1931] is shown in **Fig. 3-10**. A needle electrode was inserted in the tongue, and each subject was told to think of counting "one," "two," "three." The three deflections on the electrical tracing occurred when he thought of the three numbers. Whenever the subjects were asked to

**85**

engage in thinking activity, electrical potentials were recorded from the tongue. Even more remarkable are studies on deaf-mutes who had learned sign language [Max, 1935; Novikova, 1955]. Subjects deaf from birth and unable to speak showed electrical activity in their fingers but not their tongues during thought and when they were asleep and dreaming. Deaf children who had been taught to speak as well as use sign language showed activity in both tongue and hands. Although this type of research has not been actively pursued in recent years, it seems likely that with the sophisticated electronic technology available today it might well be possible to "read a person's mind" by recording the electrical activity of his tongue. Such evidence would seem to provide strong support for the peripheral theory of thinking.

It is important to distinguish between the extreme peripheralist position that thinking *is* small movements of the vocal apparatus and the more moderate view that such movements generally *accompany* thinking. The extremist theory was disproved in a heroic experiment in which an anesthesiologist was totally paralyzed by a form of the drug curare. As he became paralyzed, stimuli were repeatedly presented to him. He was kept totally paralyzed for a period of about 10 minutes. During that time he was conscious, mentally alert, and reported accurately the events that occurred. The protocol makes fascinating reading [Smith et al., 1947, pp. 4–8].

2:00    Electro-encephalographic and electrocardiographic continuous recording started. Control observations made on blood pressure, pulse rate and respiratory rate, neurologic signs, etc. . . .

2:11    *D*-tubocurarine chloride [the curare drug] injected intravenously at a slow constant rate so that 200 units were administered over a fifteen-minute period. Feels "a little bit dizzy and quite a 'glow.' " "A little hard to focus on anything." Weakness in jaw muscles noted. "Hard to talk." Difficulty in swallowing and keeping eyes open. "No unpleasant sensations, legs feel weak."

2:18    Upon subject's request, oxygen administration with face mask started. "Can hardly bring teeth together." Complains of residual odor from rebreathing bag. Alpha rhythm in electro-encephalogram prominent and inhibited by pattern vision. Total of 100 units *d*-tubocurarine chloride given. . . .

2:20    Speech no longer possible. Can hear distinctly. Still able to nod head and to move hands slightly, but can scarcely move fingers. . . .

2:24    Head movement impossible. Unable to open eyes. Can wrinkle forehead slightly and indicates in this manner, in response to inquiry, that he can see clearly when his eyelids are manually elevated.

2:26    Ability to comprehend and answer questions accurately is indicated by correctness of replies when the inquiries are restated in the negative or double negative. Indicates he desires the experiment to continue. Upon request, moves feet and hands slightly. Total of 200 units given. . . .

2:30    No further spontaneous respiratory movements. Ability to wrinkle forehead almost gone, but indicates he can hear, see, and feel touch and pain as well as ever. . . .

2:32    Can no longer move feet or hands upon request, and indicates by slight remaining movement of left eyebrow that he is trying to do so. . . .

2:37    Subject signals in answer to inquiries that sensorium is normal, airway is not troublesome, and painful stimuli are felt. Additional 100 units *d*-tubocurarine chloride given rapidly; total 400 units. . . .

2:42    Ability to signal by slight movement inner aspect left eyebrow almost gone. Indicates he desires the final 100 units, that he is perfectly conscious and that his sensorium is unimpaired.

2:44    Additional 100 units *d*-tubocurarine chloride given rapidly; total, 500 units. [*d*-tubocurarine discontinued at this point.]

2:45    Subject now unable to signal response to inquiries, due to complete skeletal muscular paralysis. . . .

2:48    Eyelids manually opened. Alpha rhythm of electroencephalogram inhibited by pattern vision (object held in line of gaze). Subject stated upon recovery that he was "clear as a bell" all this period. . . .

2:56    Subject can now contract muscles of medial aspect left eyebrow. Communication thus being reestablished, he signals that he can hear and see normally, and the painful stimuli are felt. . . .

3:06    Respiratory effort becoming more prominent. Extremities still completely paralyzed. Muscle of eyelids and forehead much more active. Can open eyes with difficulty. . . .

3:14    Subject indicates that he is uncomfortable when artificial respiration is even briefly discontinued. Can move his feet slightly, but not hands. Can move tongue but cannot speak. . . .

3:25    Spontaneous respirations improved. Speech is weak and slurred, but now intelligible. . . .

4:50    With assistance, subject is able to sit up on edge of bed. Complains of dizziness. Complete subjective report dictated. . . .

SUBJECTIVE REPORT    . . . The subject remained acutely conscious throughout the experiment and memory was unimpaired. At no time was there any evidence of lapse of consciousness or clouding of the sensorium. This statement is based particularly on the fact that at intervals of a minute or less, during the period when communication with the subject was impossible, various statements were made, questions asked, stimuli presented, objects placed in the line of gaze and so forth, on which the subject was requested to report when speech returned. In each instance, the report was accurate in all details and properly oriented as to temporal sequence. Indeed, several occurrences which were forgotten or unrecorded by the experimenters were recalled by the subject. Visual acuity and color sense were not affected. Vision was handicapped only by diplopia ["double vision"; since the muscles that control the eyes could not focus on a common point] and the inability to focus on anything that was not directly in line of gaze. The eyes remained passively shut most of the time. Hearing and smell were unimpaired. Indeed, it seemed to the subject that hearing was more acute than normal and remarks whispered at a distance of 20 feet were heard distinctly. Taste sensation was not examined.

This account is given at length not only because of its rather dramatic character, but because it conclusively disproves the extreme peripheralist position that thought consists in muscular movements. The subject was able to perceive and think in a relatively normal manner while his entire musculature was totally paralyzed.

We know relatively little about the neural basis of thought. It is clear that the cerebral cortex, the most recent neural structure to evolve, and the structure that has its greatest elaboration in higher primates, particularly in human beings, is essential for the development of higher mental processes. More specifically, the *association areas* of the cerebral cortex, which are neither specifically sensory nor specifically motor, are critically involved. Extensive experiments in which specific regions of association cortex were removed in monkeys, together with careful evaluation of the behavioral effects, have given us fascinating glimpses of what comparable regions of the human brain might do. Accidental brain damage in humans from injury or disease also provides "experiments of nature" that have, in the hands of skilled clinicians, given further hints of cortical function in thought. Finally, work of neurosurgeons such as Penfield, who electrically stimulates the cerebral cortex of conscious patients, has offered tantalizing suggestions about the neurology of mind. We do know something from such work about the cortical areas involved in speech and language.

The sensory and motor areas of the brain are shown in **Fig. 3-11,** along with possible functions of the association areas. A general distinction can be made between frontal and posterior association areas. The frontal cortex seems more involved in the processes that involve "thought in time," and the posterior areas are involved more in complex perception. More specifically, damage to the frontal cortex in primates produces loss of the ability to perform delayed-response tasks of the sort shown in **Fig. 3-2** [French and Harlow, 1962; Jacobsen, 1935]. Damage to the posterior association cortex, however, impairs complex visual and other sensory discriminations [Harlow, 1952; Pribram, 1954]. In particular, learning set is severely impaired after posterior lesions [Riopelle et al., 1953].

It is difficult to compare these studies on monkeys directly with effects of accidental damage in man. There do seem to be some consistencies. Pribram et al. [1964] have developed a general view, based on extensive studies with monkeys, that frontal damage results in the continued use of responses that were correct in the past, even though the same stimuli are no longer rewarded in the new situation. On the basis of extensive studies of humans with frontal damage Milner [1964] concludes that it results in a deficit in situations that require a constant shifting of response to meet changing environmental demands. Under

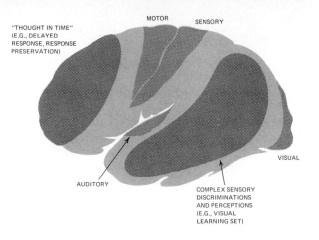

FIGURE 3-11　　*Summary of the general types of higher functions mediated by the frontal and posterior association regions of the primate brain—a greatly oversimplified schema.*

such conditions the patient seems unable to suppress his ongoing response tendencies or to rid himself of interference from previous sensory events.

There is an analog between the effects of damage to posterior association cortex in monkey and man. As we noted, complex sensory discriminations and learning set are impaired in the monkey. In man damage to comparable regions in the nondominant hemisphere—usually the right, which is not essential for speech in right-handed people—produces loss of awareness of visual-sensory orientation; such persons are often unable to orient themselves in space. Penfield provides a clear example [1969, p. 151]:

> In one patient, this area on the nondominant side was removed completely. In the years that followed the operation, the patient's epileptic attacks stopped. He was able to earn his living, but he had a penalty to pay. With his eyes closed, he had no conception of his position in space. On leaving his house in the village where he lived, he seemed to be well oriented until he turned a street corner. After that he was lost. To get back home, it was necessary for him to ask the direction from a passerby.

In a brilliant book *The Organization of Behavior,* Hebb [1949] proposed a theory of how the brain might develop neural coding of perception and concepts. In essence he suggested that during development after birth the organism learns to perceive visual objects as a result of numerous experiences with simple forms. Lines and other simple stimuli are coded by complex interconnecting groups of neurons, which he termed *cell assemblies,* and these in turn interconnect with one another in still more complex ways to form *phase sequences,* which code squares, triangles, and other more complex forms. As learning continues these processes are elaborated into very complex coding of concepts in association cortex. A somewhat different view has been developed by Konorski [1967], Thompson [1969], and others. Konorski suggested

**89**

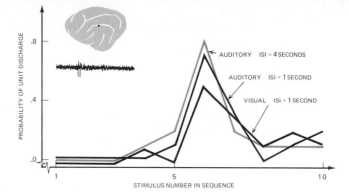

FIGURE 3–12    *A neuron in the association cortex of the cat that could serve to code the concept of number six. A series of 10 stimuli are given repeatedly, and the probability of spike discharge of the cell is plotted against stimulus number in the sequence. The cell tends to fire most on the sixth stimulus, regardless of whether the stimulus is auditory or visual and regardless of whether it is given at a rate of one every second or one every 4 seconds. ISI is the interstimulus interval, the time between successive stimuli. The location of this cell is shown by the dot in the association center of the cat brain, and the tracing is an example of the cell discharging to a "six" stimulus. [Thompson et al., 1970]*

that even very complex concepts could be represented by single neurons in the cerebral cortex which he termed *gnostic cells* (from the Greek *gnosis*, knowledge). Actually these two ideas are not contradictory. Gnostic cells could well develop through learning by means of the complex assemblages of neurons that Hebb envisaged.

The work of Hubel and Wiesel [1959] seems to support the idea that single neurons code concepts, at least in visual perception. It is known that the single neurons in the visual cortex code angles and forms, and this coding is apparently present at birth. In a very real sense these visual form-coding cells are "concept," or "gnostic," cells; they respond to a category of stimuli in the same sense that human subjects learn to respond to a category such as triangle in simple concept-learning experiments (see Fig. 3-6). Even more complex types of concept-coding cells have been reported in recent times. For example, Gross et al. [1969] described a neuron in the posterior association cortex of the monkey that responded only to a form resembling a monkey's hand; the more the stimulus silhouette resembled a hand, the more the cell fired. This might be termed a "hand-concept" gnostic cell.

Thompson et al. [1970] have observed cells in the association cortex of the cat that could serve to code the concept of number. In the example shown in Fig. 3-12, series of stimuli were presented, one after the other, and the cell fired mostly on the sixth presentation. This was independent of the nature of the stimulus (sound or light), the intensity of the stimulus, and the time between successive stimuli. The response was only in terms of the number of stimuli. One cell of this number-coding type was even found in a very young kitten, suggesting that such cells may function as a result of an innate mechanism. As we saw in connection with human concept-learning experiments, color, shape, and number seem to form an increasingly difficult series of concepts. Color is coded at the level of the eye, while form is coded at the level of the visual cortex, and number may be coded in the association cortex. It is important to keep in mind that the evidence regarding such concept-coding or gnostic neurons is still preliminary and tentative. There are single neurons in the cerebral cortex that *could* serve to code angle, hand, and number, but it remains to be determined whether or not such neurons are in fact performing these functions. We stand at the very beginning in our knowledge of how the human brain, the most complex structure in the universe, can develop concepts and ideas.

## LANGUAGE AND COMMUNICATION

Language is unique to man. Every human society possesses language. The development of all human culture has been possible only through the use of language. Language has provided the vehicle for an entirely new kind of evolution. Until the appearance of the language-using animal called man, animals adapted to their environments or they perished. With the development of the ability to transmit ideas and knowledge through language, man reversed evolution and began to adapt the environment to his own needs. In fact, in view of the present rate of increase in environmental pollution and ecological imbalance, man may gain the dubious distinction of being the only species to have adapted the environment to the point of engineering his own destruction.

We must make a fundamental distinction between language and communication. Only man possesses *language*, but many species of animals *communicate* and some, such as the parrot, can even emit clear speech sounds. However, the parrot can never learn to combine words in a meaningful way; it cannot develop syntax. Language has both grammar and syntax. *Grammar* refers to all the rules for correct use of a language, and *syntax* refers to that part of grammar concerned with the ordering of words, as in a sentence. Young children, who may possess a vocabulary smaller than that of a well-trained parrot, are able to generate meaningful *new* sentences, sentences they have not learned before as such, with appropriate use of syntax.

Communication among members of a species seems to be more a rule than an exception. At a very simple level *species-specific* communication involves the release of chemicals called *pheromones*, which serve as signals. The female Bombyx moth, when ready to mate, releases an odor that can be detected by the male as much as 7 miles away. This odor signals that she is ready and willing, and because of the way the male odor receptors function, it also provides information about where she is. The male receptors are extremely sensitive to very weak concentrations of the odor but respond differentially only to much higher concentrations. Since moths tend to fly against the wind, the male will approach the vicinity of the female simply by flying. When he is close the higher concentration of the odor provides differential cues that

**91**

guide him to the female. This, of course, is an extremely simple form of communication. Communication in the honeybee is a much more striking example; as noted in **Chapter 4,** when a foraging bee discovers nectar, he returns to the hive and performs a dance that communicates to the other bees the direction and distance to the food.

Communication is not necessarily species specific, particularly in higher animals. A baboon troop in search of food will often stay with a herd of zebras, and the alarm given by either species at the approach of a lion is correctly interpreted by both the zebras and the baboons. Some forms of communication seem to be shared among primates and are perhaps order specific. For example, the beckoning gesture with the hand and arm apparently means "come here" to wild chimpanzees as well as to men.

Examples of both intraspecies and interspecies communication are numberless. However, there are as yet no really convincing demonstrations that any species other than man has developed the specialized aspect of communication we call language. Chimpanzee tribes in the wild state show a wide variety of vocalizations that serve to communicate information, but the sounds appear to be species specific and not much dependent on learning. Human language is eminently learned. There are several hundred different human languages, many of them totally unrelated. They are not even limited to spoken word sounds. The bushmen in Africa developed a language consisting in large part of clicks, still other cultures developed whistle languages, and American Indians developed a sign language. The extent to which language is a result of the uniquely complex development of the human animal is a critical, and as yet unanswered, question. The fact that every human society or group, no matter how primitive, isolated, or culturally backward it may appear, has developed a complete and complex language suggests that language development is a necessary, perhaps even genetically determined, result of possessing a human brain.

One approach to this question is to attempt to teach language to nonhuman primates. Among the primates the gorilla has the largest brain next to man, but there are certain practical difficulties involved in raising a gorilla in the home. The chimpanzee has been most widely studied and seems a very good choice. He exhibits social behavior resembling that of man, he is our closest living relative in terms of biochemical criteria such as blood type and characteristics, and he is roughly similar in size. There have been several attempts to teach chimps to learn spoken language. The most notable was the effort of Hayes and Hayes, who raised a chimp named Vikki from birth to the age of six in their home. Vikki's social and emotional development were strikingly similar to that of a human child; indeed, the Hayes treated her as much in this manner as possible. They spent a great deal of time attempting to teach Vikki to speak, much more time than parents normally devote to such efforts. The results were conclusively negative. Vikki learned to speak only four words, and these were not clearly pronounced. Does this constitute complete failure to learn language? Actually Vikki's failure was in speaking, not necessarily in understanding. Vikki learned to communicate a good deal by gestures and expressions, and she evidently understood a great deal more than she could speak. Of course in terms of understanding and responding correctly to words, dogs can be trained to understand well over 100 separate verbal commands. Vikki used different gestures accompanying her few spoken words with sufficient consistency that outside observers watching movies of her performance could understand what she said equally well with and without the sound track. [Hayes, 1951; Hayes and Hayes, 1951].

The results of the Hayes' study, which showed clearly that chimpanzees cannot be taught to speak language, suggested that language as it is used by man is an exclusively human ability. This conclusion was widely accepted until very recently. There are several alternative explanations why chimpanzees cannot be taught to speak. Perhaps the most obvious is the possibility that their peripheral vocal apparatus is unsuited to speech. This is not clearly known. However, wild chimps produce a large variety of vocalizations, and humans with extensive throat surgery are able to speak intelligibly; thus chimps ought to be able to do so, even if pronunciation is imperfect. In any event, a proper vocal apparatus is clearly not a sufficient condition for language; parrots can speak words quite clearly, but they cannot learn language. This suggests a second possibility that chimpanzees simply do not have sufficient intellectual ability to learn language.

Such has been the general conclusion until the very recent and important work by Gardner and Gardner [1969; 1970]. They reasoned that perhaps chimpanzees did have the intellectual capacity for language, but not in terms of *vocal* behavior. Both wild chimps and chimps raised in captivity make very similar vocal sounds, suggesting that perhaps their "verbal" behavior is species specific—that is, genetically determined— and not much subject to influence or change; another way of putting it would be that the verbal behavior of chimps is not very plastic. The Gardners noted, however, that chimps use their hands with great skill—a chimp can do almost any manual task a man can do—and consequently it might be possible to teach a chimp sign language. The Gardners have succeeded in doing just this. Their report is fascinating reading. Their subject, Washoe, was less than ideal in that she was over a year old when they obtained her and had been captured wild. Instead of raising Washoe in their house, they set up a trailer-house apartment with a bedroom, kitchen, bathroom, living room, and a large outdoor play area. One of the experimenters was with Washoe from the time she got up in the morning until bedtime, but she spent the nights alone. From the beginning the experimenters refrained from using words and used only American Sign Language to "talk" to Washoe. They were not bound to any one type of training or learning-theory approach, but tried everything, including contingent reinforcement, shaping, demonstration (to provide opportunity for imitative learning), and directed training, whereby they simply held Washoe's hands and fingers in correct positions. Interestingly enough, the last approach, together with imitation, was the most

**93**

FIGURE 3-13    *Washoe "saying" words in American Sign Language. Left, Washoe fingerpainting. Above, Washoe making the sign for drink. Pictures taken in December 1967, when Washoe was two and one-half.* [Gardner and Gardner, University of Nevada, Reno]

successful, and reinforcement of spontaneous behavior was the least successful, which may surprise reinforcement-learning theorists but will come as no surprise to parents.

At the age of three Washoe had a vocabulary of nearly 100 words, including nouns, verbs, and pronouns. She used the signs spontaneously and appropriately, used them correctly in new situations, and generalized to similar objects and events. She spoke up to six-word sentences, and used subjects, verbs, objects, and pronouns in the correct sequences. In short, she has learned American Sign Language and apparently rather well when compared to a three-year-old human child deaf from birth. Linguists will no doubt argue for some time about the extent to which Washoe has actually developed language. The reader may judge for himself in the following excerpts from her language behavior [Gardner and Gardner, 1971]:

A listing of Washoe's phrases, together with the contexts in which they occurred, is striking because the phrases seem so apt. For play with her companions, she would sign *Roger you tickle, you Greg peekaboo,* or simply, *catch me* or *tickle me.* She indicated destinations with phrases such as *go in, go out,* or *in down bed.* Other phrases produced descriptions: *drink red* for her red cup, *my baby* for her dolls, *listen eat* or *listen drink* for the supper bell, and *dirty good* for the toilet chair. Asking for access to the many objects that were kept out of sight and out of reach by the various locked doors in her quarters, Washoe signed, *key open food* at the refrigerator, *open key clean* at the soap cupboard, and *key open please blanket* at the bedding cupboard. Combinations with *sorry* were frequent, and these were appropriate for apology and irresistible as appeasements: *please sorry, sorry dirty, sorry hurt, please sorry good,* and *come hug sorry sorry.*

Any participant in this project saw and responded to *go out* and *tickle me* far more often than he cared to remember. Soda pop, which Washoe referred to as *sweet drink,* was requested by all the following: *please sweet drink, more sweet drink, gimmie sweet drink, hurry sweet drink, please hurry sweet drink, please gimmie sweet drink,* and by variations in the order of these signs. . . .

About half of the longer combinations were formed by adding appeal-signs to shorter combinations, as in *please tickle more, come Roger tickle,* and *out open please hurry.* In the remaining cases, the additional signs introduced new information and new relations among signs. Most of the signs added were proper names or pronouns. Sometimes the effect was to specify more than one agent as in *you me in, you me out, you me Greg go,* and *Roger Washoe out. . . . You me drink go* and *you me out look* are examples of combinations which specify agent, action, and a destination or object. There were also apologies such as *hug me good,* which specified an action, an agent, and an attribute. Finally, a number of Washoe's combinations specified both the subject and the object of an action, as in *Roger Washoe tickle, you tickle me Washoe,* and *you peekaboo me.*

An example of Washoe's "speech" is shown in Fig. 3-13.

Premack [1970] has also succeeded in teaching chimpanzees language, using a quite different approach. He employed little plastic cut-out forms to represent words. For example, a blue triangle is the sign for "apple." The chimp must place a blue triangle on a board in order to obtain an apple. His star pupil, a seven-year-old chimp named Sarah, now has a vocabulary of over 120 words, including common and proper nouns, abstract nouns for concepts, verbs, adjectives, adverbs, and uses them appropriately in sentences. The work of the Gardners and Premack would seem to settle the issue; chimpanzees can learn language.

## PSYCHOLINGUISTICS

Of all human activities, language seems among the most obviously learned. A young child can learn any language with equal facility. There are well over 2000 different languages in use in the world today and many more that have disappeared completely. Linguistics, the formal study of language, has in part been an effort to bring order into this seeming chaos. Many languages, such as Portuguese and Spanish or Danish and Swedish, are clearly very closely related. Over and above these obvious similarities it appears that there are large families of related languages. The best known of these is Indo-European, which includes virtually all modern languages of the Western world—English, French, German, Spanish, Italian, Russian, the Scandanavian group, and so on. Interestingly, Sanskrit, the ancient literary and religious language of India, is also a member of the Indo-European group, but Finnish,

Hungarian, and Basque are not. Languages are grouped in families according to similarities in morphology and syntax. In the case of the Indo-European languages, rules have been developed which permit correct prediction of the form of the root word in virtually all Indo-European languages. By use of these rules linguists have constructed "Proto-Indo-European," the original "language" from which all other Indo-European languages developed. For example, English *wheel* and Russian *koleso* both trace to Indo-European *kwelos*, which in turn can be retraced to English *cycle* through Greek *kuklos*. *Beef* and *cow* come originally from Indo-European *gwous*, one through Latin *bōs, bovis,* and the other through Old English *cū*. All Indo-European languages have common words for natural phenomena—*night, star, dew, snow, wind, thunder,* and *fire*; for animals—*hound, goat, ewe, ox, steer,* and *sow*; for parts of a house—*door, timber,* and *thatch*; for primary family relationships—*father, mother, brother,* and *sister*; and for parts of the human body.

These common words evoke an interesting picture of the primitive common culture from which Western civilization may have developed [Potter, 1960]. Indo-European may never have existed as a single language, but dialects very like it apparently did. It was originally localized to a small region of southern Russia and spread throughout much of the Western world. Approximately half the world's population now speaks one or another of the Indo-European languages; the next largest language group is Sino-Tibetan.

Modern English has roughly 40 different elementary speech sounds, or *phonemes*. Most other modern languages also have about this number of basic sounds. The sounds may, of course, be quite different in different languages—so much so that it is impossible for most adults learning a second language to master pronunciation completely. The next largest unit of analysis of language is the *morpheme*, the smallest units of speech that have meaning. Words are made up of one or more morphemes. In English the 40 phonemes are combined into a vocabulary of approximately 1 million words. In spite of this enormous potential vocabulary, 60 percent of the average person's speech consists of 120 words. Indeed, language is extremely redundant and predictable. A great many common words can be omitted, particularly when they are used in certain sequences, without any loss of meaning or communication.

Our immediate concern here is the manner in which human beings acquire and use language, the field of *psycholinguistics*. The more traditional approach in psychology stems from reinforcement learning theory, most elaborately treated by Skinner [1957]. The basic idea is that as the young infant babbles random speech sounds his parents and others around him reinforce certain of these sounds that resemble the appropriate language words. Hence the infant develops a simple approximate vocabulary, and by the same principle comes to use simple sentences. Skinner notes that the earliest statements of the child are in the nature of commands or demands, which he terms *mands*. These are generally subject to rather immediate reinforcement; "bata" results in the child's

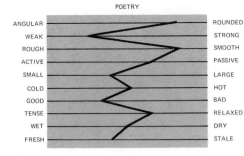

POETRY

| ANGULAR | ROUNDED |
| WEAK | STRONG |
| ROUGH | SMOOTH |
| ACTIVE | PASSIVE |
| SMALL | LARGE |
| COLD | HOT |
| GOOD | BAD |
| TENSE | RELAXED |
| WET | DRY |
| FRESH | STALE |

FIGURE 3-14    *The ratings made by a single subject for the meaning of the word "poetry" on a standard Semantic Differential Form [Deese, 1970].*

getting his bottle. At a somewhat later stage the child becomes more influenced by social approval, via reinforcement sequences, and learns responses that have a more subtle relationship to the world. These are termed *tacts*, from verbal contact with the world. The third and more complex class of utterances in Skinner's theory is the *intraverbal*—statements or terms that become conditioned to verbal stimuli. As an oversimplified example, "ball!" from a young child is a mand meaning "I want the ball"; "ball red" may be a simple tact describing a ball; and in "ball round," "round" might be an intraverbal. Skinner envisages the development of adult language from these elementary phenomena and the overriding influence of reinforcement—that is, reward and non-reward—first direct and later social. It is not possible to do justice to Skinner's interesting treatment here; he derives at least some features of the real complexity of adult language from these simple principles.

A somewhat different form of reinforcement-theory approach to one aspect of language, the nature of meaning, is Osgood's [1952] *mediation theory* of meaning, derived in part from Clark Hull's reinforcement theory of learning. It is not a general theory of language, but rather an analysis of connotative meaning—a way of measuring what words connote or signify to people. It is not fundamentally different from Skinner's view concerning reinforcement. However, Osgood assumes that some fraction of the learned verbal response to a specific object stimulus can later be made independently of the stimulus—that is, this fraction has abstract meaning. Large-scale rating studies of words led to the development of what Osgood calls the *semantic differential.* The meaning of words can be classified as *evaluative*—good-bad, beautiful-ugly, pleasant-unpleasant; *activity*—fast-slow, active-passive; and *potency*—strong-weak, masculine-feminine, hard-soft. The learned meaning of a word can be determined by its rating on each of these three dimensions. In actually rating a word, the subject judges it on a number of scales, as indicated in **Fig. 3-14,** and the three dimensions are then derived by statistical analysis. These three dimensions of meaning seem to occur in the major Indo-European languages and many Oriental tongues as well. The semantic differential is not only a useful device for analyzing how people evaluate words, but also appears to provide some insight into what it is that people mean by "meaning."

A quite different view of the genesis of language has been developed by some modern linguists, particularly Chomsky [1957; 1965;

**97**

1968]. According to this *generative theory*, characterized as *the* psycho-linguistics by some of its disciples, a universal language—or, more properly, a deep structure of universal syntax—exists in all men, and all specific languages are merely variations on this underlying theme or language structure. In essence, this view holds that we can learn much in general terms about the human mind by the study of the universal deep structure of language [Deese, 1970, pp. 10–11]:

Consider the hapless child trying to learn the sounds of his native language. How can he possibly learn to distinguish among speech sounds by their physical characteristics when carefully trained adults cannot do so under the best of laboratory conditions? In fact, the child does not simply discriminate among the speech sounds he hears. He invents a distinction and then, as a kind of hypothesis, applies that distinction to the signals he hears. If his hypothesis makes order among the signals he hears, he accepts that distinction as part of the language he is to "acquire."

From where do these invented distinctions arise? From a theory of language, or from a universal grammar? A child has as part of his native equipment a device embodying a linguistic theory of a high degree of complexity. That device enables him to perform analyses of the sounds that he hears. By applying the theory he possesses he can form an account of the language he hears in his particular culture. Eventually he learns how to interpret the language of his culture and to use it himself. It is clear that this process is not what we ordinarily mean by learning.

That children must have some inborn capacity for linguistic analysis is astounding, of course, and seems too radical for some psychologists to accept. At times this notion has been misinterpreted; it sometimes has been interpreted to suggest that each child has an inborn capacity for a particular language, or an inborn ability to speak a certain language. The capacity is aroused by the speech of adults, much as certain instinctive acts in young animals are aroused by stimuli provided by their parents. In fact, however, something much more abstract and difficult than language itself is innate. It is something that is best described as a universal grammar or as a device for producing language.

Because a universal grammar is innate, the study of grammar occupies a central position in modern psycholinguistic studies. While meaning, stylistic variations in use of language, and other matters are important, the basic concern of psycholinguistics is the nature of grammar, particularly those aspects of grammar that are universal. Some aspects of grammar are universal for superficial reasons. These are respects in which languages are alike simply as a matter of historical accident or for some other superficial reason. There are, in addition, deep reasons why all languages have basically the same structure, and these are of central importance to the psychology of language.

The generative theory of language does not mean to imply that there is or was some original universal language spoken by all primitive mankind, although scholars of a much earlier day did seriously consider this possibility. King James I of England proposed, with characteristic directness, to settle the issue by having a group of newborn infants raised on an uninhabited island of the Hebrides with a deaf-and-dumb Scottish nanny. His own opinion was that the children would all grow up to speak Hebrew. What generative theory does imply is a kind of universal syntax, the deep grammatical structure which shapes all languages.

Much of the evidence for the generative theory comes from very complex linguistic analyses [Chomsky, 1968; Deese, 1970]; there have been few experimental studies as yet. In one study Mehler and Carey [1967] compared the perception of sentences that differ in surface structure and those that differ in deep structure. For example, "John is easy to please" and "It is easy to please John" have the same deep grammatical structure, but differing surface structure, whereas "John is easy to please" and "John is eager to please" have the same surface structure but differ in deep structure. When subjects were given a series of sentences having the same deep structure and then one sentence having a different deep structure, the difference was more difficult to perceive than differences in surface structure. Experiments with children are perhaps more convincing. Deese [1970] has reviewed studies on linguistic performance of Japanese, English, and Russian children at comparable stages of language development and finds that although the adult languages differ markedly, children develop basically the same simplified deep structure in early language use. For example, English has a relatively fixed word order and Russian does not, but both English and Russian children develop initially the same simple fixed word order. In a careful observational analysis of the child's acquisition of grammar between the ages of one and three, Brown and Bellugi [1964] demonstrated that children develop the general rules for speaking English without training. An example familiar to all parents is the use of regular forms for irregular verbs, "I digged a hole!" Children know the rule for forming the past tense of words such as "dig" even though it has not been taught, and they persist in applying it even after numerous corrections. Brown and Bellugi conclude that "the very intricate simultaneous differentiation and integration that constitutes the evolution of the noun phrase is more reminiscent of the biological development of an embryo than it is of the acquisition of a conditioned reflex."

## THE NEURAL BASIS OF LANGUAGE

The generative theory of language, to the extent that it is true, has interesting implications for the neural basis of language; there must be an innate biological representation of the abstract structures of language wired into the brain. Lenneberg [1967] has discussed the biological foundations of language and develops some of the evidence for the view that there is no inherent variation in the basic characteristics of human language. Although particular sounds differ in different languages, each language has about 40 different sounds. The deep structure of all languages is the same. All children appear to develop the same initial universal deep grammar. In addition, there is no evidence of evolution or development of languages. All languages have the same degree of complexity; of course, they change over time, but they do not tend to become either more simple or more complex as a result of such changes.

A most important indirect kind of evidence concerns the plasticity of language development in children. A young child can learn a second language with no trace of an accent; an adult cannot. Even more important, if the dominant hemisphere for speech (the left hemisphere for the right-handed) is damaged in the young child, he will subsequently develop perfectly normal speech. However, if the damage occurs after about the age of twelve, he will have some degree of permanent speech defect.

Perhaps the most informative evidence about the biological basis of language comes from the study of *aphasia*, impairment of language behavior following brain damage. Although authorities disagree on the details of localization of the speech areas in the human cortex, the overall picture seems clear [Penfield, 1969]. A diagram of the dominant hemisphere of the human brain is shown in **Fig. 3-15**, it is damage on the dominant side that produces aphasia. Although this is always the left hemisphere in right-handed people, it may be either the left or the right hemisphere in left-handed persons. This is itself an intriguing fact, since the early signs of handedness and language development seem to occur at about the same time in infancy. However, there is not an invariable correspondence in the development of the individual. For example, if there is injury in early childhood to the left cortical hand area which controls the right hand, the child becomes left-handed, but the speech area remains in the left hemisphere. There may, however, be a correspondence between hand use and the development of language in evolutionary terms.

Of the three speech areas in the dominant hemisphere, the superior area is the least important. Aphasia following its removal does not continue for more than a few weeks. The anterior speech area, discovered by Broca, is next in importance and lies just anterior to and below the region of the motor cortex controlling tongue and throat (anatomical representation in Fig. 3-15). Removal of this area results in severe aphasia, but it generally clears up over a period of months to years in the adult. Removal of the posterior speech cortex, *Warnicke's area*, which forms a large portion of the posterior association cortex in the dominant hemisphere, results in permanent aphasia in adults.

The effects of damage to these regions in young children are dramatically different. If the posterior speech area is destroyed before the age of twelve, the child who has already developed language will become completely aphasic, but after about a year he will begin to speak again and will in all likelihood learn language perfectly. After the age of twelve there is no relearning of speech. Note that this corresponds to the age limit for learning a second language without accent.

Electrical stimulation of the dominant-hemisphere speech areas in the conscious adult produces a temporary aphasia that lasts only as

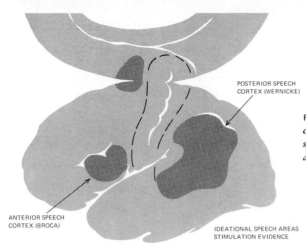

POSTERIOR SPEECH
CORTEX (WERNICKE)

FIGURE 3-15 *Speech areas of the
cerebral cortex in the dominant hemisphere of the human brain. [Penfield
and Roberts, 1959]*

ANTERIOR SPEECH
CORTEX (BROCA)

IDEATIONAL SPEECH AREAS
STIMULATION EVIDENCE

long as the stimulus is applied. The electrical stimulus acts as an interference with normal function in these areas. This contrasts with the effects of stimulating the sensory cortex; if the visual area is so stimulated,
the subject does not report interference with vision, but instead sees
"lights." Localization of the speech areas mapped out by electrical-
stimulation-produced aphasia agrees well with the evidence from the
effects of brain damage.

The area in the *non*dominant hemisphere that corresponds to the
posterior speech area is not normally involved in language behavior, but
rather seems to be involved in awareness of spatial relations. Research
has indicated that these areas in both monkey and man seem to
subserve complex visual discriminations. Penfield [1969] discovered
that when a young child learns to speak again after destruction of the
speech area in the dominant hemisphere, the speech mechanism is found
newly established in the speech area of the other hemisphere. It is as
though in normal development the posterior association area in one
hemisphere develops the neural substrate of language and the same area
on the other side comes to code spatial relations. After these differing
functions have been developed, they cannot be changed.

The fact that the essential speech area is limited to a particular region
of association cortex in one hemisphere has significant implications
concerning the neural basis of language. Many authorities believe complex learning involves the entire nervous system—at least the higher regions, including the cerebral cortex. However, the most important and
complex learning man does, the learning of language, seems to be coded
in a very specific area. Language learning may differ fundamentally from
other forms of learning. The generative theory of language implies a
genetically determined neuronal matrix which provides a universal grammar for all mankind. The structural basis of such a universal grammar
may exist in the predetermined organization of the posterior speech area
of the human cerebral cortex.

**101**

THOUGHT AND LANGUAGE

# SUMMARY

Thought and language are, indeed, the most complex and important activities of man. The study of thinking includes two broad areas of research—nondirected thought and directed thought, such as problem solving and concept formation. The more general aspects of thinking include the distinction between conscious and unconscious thought processes. Daydreaming and fantasy, aspects of nondirected thought, can be categorized with regard to content as general, self-recriminating, objective, poorly controlled, autistic, and neurotic. Autistic thought, which characterizes schizophrenia, is typically disordered and illogical. Directed thinking occurs even in such lowly animals as the rat, as evidenced by the delayed-reaction task. However, more complex types of solutions, as in the *umweg* problem or *learning set*, occur only in higher animals. Concepts can be developed by lower animals as well as by man. They may develop extremely rapidly, as in insight learning, or only with much problem-solving practice, as in learning the concept of oddity.

Human conceptual behavior involves the use of strategies, or conceptual rules, in order to group or categorize objects or experiences on the basis of stimulus attributes. Examples include the conjunctive rule, in which two stimulus attributes define the correct concept; the disjunctive rule, which requires one or another attribute for the correct concept; and a relational rule, which requires a comparison of stimuli independent of absolute stimulus attributes. Another type of strategy is the TOTE system, in which incoming perceptual data are compared to existing hypotheses. The related phenomena of problem solving involve strategies such as deductive and inductive logic to arrive at the solutions to problems. Computer simulation of problem solving promises to provide interesting examples of the way in which human problem solving takes place.

Theories of thought emphasize peripheral or central processes. The extreme peripheral theory, suggesting that thought is nothing more than subvocal speech, has been discounted by the evidence that even a completely paralyzed person is capable of thinking. It appears that the association areas of the cerebral cortex are intimately involved in higher mental processes, with the frontal regions more involved in thought in time and the posterior regions involved in complex sensory discriminations and learning set. Simple concepts or perceptions may be coded by single cells in these areas, by groups of cells, or by both. Interwoven with the study of thought processes is the study of language and its development. Communication among members of a species may take the form of release of chemical pheromones, elaborate movements and gestures, or vocalizations. Many types of communication can be understood by more than a single species, although language as understood and used by humans cannot be learned by other animals, except perhaps in a nonvocal form such as sign language.

The formal study of language, linguistics, has revealed many similarities among the more than 2000 different languages in use today.

The largest and best known family of related languages, the Indo-European family, includes most of the modern languages of the Western world. The study of the way in which humans acquire and use language is called psycholinguistics. Reinforcement theorists have argued that the acquisition of patterns of communication is shaped and maintained by reinforcement from parents and others around the child. According to the mediation theory of meaning, the meanings of words (responses) are to some extent independent of the objects they might represent. The semantic differential analyzes these meanings into three broad categories—evaluative, activity, and potency. The generative theory of language development suggests that there is a universal deep grammatical structure in all human language.

The study of aphasia has provided evidence that specific areas of the brain control language. Damage to one of the three speech areas on the dominant side of the cerebral hemispheres causes aphasia, which may be permanent, as in the case of damage to the posterior speech area, or temporary, as in the case of damage to the superior speech area or the anterior speech area.

## CHAPTER FOUR

### INTELLIGENCE AND INTELLIGENT BEHAVIOR

In a sense we all know what the word "intelligence" means. You may have concluded that some of your friends are more intelligent than others. You probably know some people who have achieved distinction because of their intelligence. You may know of some who have such low intelligence that they have to be kept in an institution for the mentally retarded. You may also share the generally accepted view that human beings are more intelligent than apes, who are more intelligent than cats and dogs, who in turn are more intelligent than slugs or sponges. On what basis do we make these judgments? It is "obvious" that some people are more intelligent than others, but exactly what is it that is obvious? Certainly intelligence is not an observable attribute, like body size and form. It is one thing to say that cats and dogs have more hair than sponges; it is another thing to say that they are more intelligent.

Since the word "intelligence" is a noun it is easy to fall into the trap of thinking of intelligence as some "thing" which causes individuals to behave intelligently. Intelligence is not a thing. Individual men and

# INTELLIGENCE

beasts differ in the degree to which their *behavior* is intelligent, just as they differ in height and weight. However, height and weight do not *cause* stature; they merely describe it. In the same sense, intelligence is not the *cause* of intelligent behavior; it is merely a term we use to refer to certain features of an individual's behavior. Just as stature is determined by many influences, including genetics, nutrition, disease, and injury, so intelligent behavior is a result of many influences. We assume that intelligence is a function of the brain and that the various factors which determine intelligence do so through their influences on the development and functioning of the central nervous system. In this chapter we shall examine some of the bases of individual differences in intelligence in man and the other animals.

There are many definitions of intelligence, each emphasizing a different feature of behavior. The problem lies in specifying exactly what intelligent behavior is. Is it, as some definitions suggest, the capacity for abstract thinking, or is it simply the ability to learn? The most useful definition, as well as the least satisfactory from a theoretical standpoint, is that intelligence is what is tested by an intelligence test. However, you do not need to know the results of an intelligence test to make a judgment about someone's intelligence. Furthermore, you may feel, perhaps with some justification, that the performance measured by an intelligence test is not what *you* mean by intelligence. This is the basic reason there is no universally accepted definition of intelligence. It is also why studies of the nature and bases of intelligence have not awaited a definition.

Until the publication of Darwin's influential book *The Origin of Species* [1859], we human beings regarded ourselves as quite different from the other animals. In fact, the term "animal" is still used interchangeably with "infrahuman." Until quite recently even the causes of behavior were thought to be different in humans and infrahumans. All lower animals were believed to be endowed with instincts, while man was endowed with reason. Acceptance of the idea that species, including man, evolved from other species required a rejection, or at least a re-examination, of this view. If evolution is a continual process, then man and other animals must be at least somewhat similar in behavior as well as in anatomy and physiology. In a subsequent, less well-known book *The Expression of the Emotions in Man and Animals* Darwin [1872] attempted to show that many of our emotional responses, such as facial expressions and blushing, are similar to those seen in lower animals. Darwin clearly needed some such evidence of continuity in some aspects of behavior. At the same time one of Darwin's friends, Romanes, collected evidence of humanlike behavior in lower animals, which he published in the book *Animal Intelligence* [1895]. Since animal behavior had not yet been subjected to extensive scientific investigation, Romanes was forced to rely on the reports of "reliable observers." Some of these reports may cause the reader to wonder about the intelligence, and even the sanity, of the "reliable observers." In some cases the observations appear to be more like hallucinations. The following is a typical example [Romanes, 1895, p. 364]:

Powelsen, a writer on Iceland, has related an account of the intelligence displayed by the mice of that country, which has given rise to a difference of competent opinion, and which perhaps can hardly yet be said to have been definitely settled. What Powelsen said is that the mice collect in parties of from six to ten, select a flat piece of dried cow-dung, pile berries or other food upon it, then with united strength drag it to the edge of any stream they wish to cross, launch it, embark, and range themselves round the central heap of provisions with their heads joined over it, and their tails hanging in the water, perhaps serving as rudders. [Since this observation was met with considerable skepticism, one investigator] . . . therefore, determined on trying to arrive at the truth of the matter, with the following result:—"I made a point of inquiring of different individuals as to the reality of the account, and am happy in being able to say that it is now established as an important fact in natural history by the testimony of two eyewitnesses of unquestionable veracity, the clergyman of Briamslaek, and Madame Benedictson of Stickesholm, both of whom assured me that they had seen the expedition performed repeatedly. Madame Benedictson, in particular, recollected having spent a whole afternoon, in her younger days, at the margin of a small lake on which these skillful navigators had embarked, and amusing herself and her companions by driving them away from the sides of the lake as they approached them.

Although mice may not be capable of displaying intelligent behavior of this particular type, research conducted since the time of Romanes has provided extensive evidence that infrahumans are capable of quite complex behavior which involves problem solving, or reasoning.

Infrahumans are not mere bundles of instincts and man is not completely rational, but there is little doubt that in terms of intelligence man is at the top of the phylogenetic pile. We do not yet know the basis of this superior intelligence. We assume that our brains are "better" than those of infrahumans, but we do not yet know exactly what structures and neurobiological functions of our brains make us more intelligent. We assume that we are more intelligent because of our abilities to plan, invent, solve problems, use language, develop culture, and create and appreciate art. We do not differ from other animals simply because we can learn; this is a capacity we share with most, if not all, animals. Insects and even protozoa are quite capable of some types of learning. Higher animals appear to differ from lower ones in terms of the complexity of the tasks that they are able to learn. The ability to learn is essential for intelligent behavior, but learning is not synonymous with intelligence.

Of course, it is our own view of intelligence that places man at the top of the evolutionary pile. Intelligence is sometimes defined as the ability to adapt to the requirements of an environment. In this sense all processes that contribute to adaptation, such as the growing of white hair by arctic animals, are "intelligent." Of course this is tantamount to defining intelligence as the process of evolution. There is nothing inherently wrong with such a definition. However, in this chapter we are considering intelligence in a more restricted sense, as the nature of and the processes underlying intelligent behavior in individual animals.

By implicit general agreement *instincts*, the complex genetically influenced responses of species which develop without specific training, are excluded from the concept of intelligence as we are considering it here. Such responses are, of course, "intelligent" in an evolutionary sense, as the following example shows. In a series of brilliant experiments Von Frisch and other workers [Lindauer, 1961; Wenner, 1964] discovered how honeybees returning from a food source communicate the location of the food to other bees in the colony. When they return to the hive the bees perform an agitated "dance" on the face of the combs inside the hive. Some of the findings are shown in Fig. 4-1. The speed of dancing is closely correlated with the distance of the food source. The direction of the food source is indicated by the vertical direction of

**107**

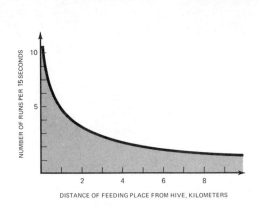

FIGURE 4-1 *Dance of honeybees. Honeybees returning from a food source dance on the vertical surface of the honeycomb inside the hive. Speed of the dance decreases with the distance of the food source. This is the round dance; the waggle dance, indicated by the wavy lines, communicates the direction of the food source in relation to the sun. If the source is in the direction of the sun, the dance is vertical; if it is 60 degrees to the left of the direction of the sun, the waggle dance is 60 degrees to the left of vertical.* [Von Frisch, 1953]

a portion of the dance called the "waggle dance." The bees also emit different sounds during different phases of the dance. Thus they "show and tell" in a rather abstract language. Moreover, different species of bees speak different dialects. A species of Italian bees indicates direction of food with a form of dance entirely different from the one shown here.

There is much about this type of communication that we do not yet understand. What causes the bee to perform the intricate dance when it returns to the hive? How do other bees in the colony know what the signals mean? This highly interesting communication has been described, but we do not yet understand its bases. From the colony's perspective such communication is highly intelligent, but bee language is not like our language in that it consists only of very specific signals. The fact that different species of bees perform different dances suggests that the pattern of the dance is genetically controlled. In contrast, although our genetic endowment allows for the development of language, the particular language we speak is not genetically determined. We have the ability to acquire any language that is spoken around us, and we can communicate an almost infinite amount of information through language. Man's linguistic abilities must thus be regarded as one indication of greater intelligence.

## MEASURES OF INTELLIGENCE

Since it has proved so difficult to develop an acceptable definition of intelligence, it seems that it would be even more difficult to measure intellectual performance. However, as you know from your own experience intelligence tests have become a standard part of the armamentarium of modern education. Before the turn of the century there were no intelligence tests. The first systematic attempts to measure mental functioning were made by Francis Galton, Darwin's cousin. During the 1880s Galton maintained a laboratory in London where, for a small fee, he measured visitors on a variety of simple psychological tests for color vision, reaction time, and hearing acuity. The differences

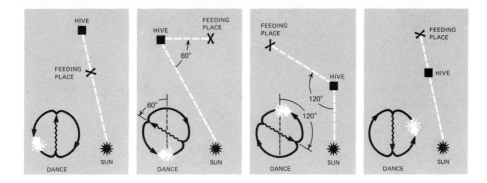

in individual performance even in these simple tasks was striking. Early tests developed by others, such as Cattell [1890], were also based on simple measures of perceptual judgment or speed of reaction.

The difficulty with these early attempts was that they provided highly reliable measures of highly uninteresting responses. Most of us would not regard speed of response as a measure of intellectual prowess. It was clear even then that tests of intelligence must measure more complex mental functioning. The first systematic efforts in this direction were made by the great French psychologist Alfred Binet. Binet and his associates attempted to develop tests of such complex abilities as memory, imagination, attention, comprehension, suggestibility, esthetic appreciation, persistence, moral sentiments, motor skill, and judgment of visual space. Binet also tried to determine which tests provided measures that showed improvement with age and related closely to school achievement. In other words, Binet attempted to see if his tests were *valid*—if they tested what they were supposed to test, intellectual performance. Obviously, even a test that is highly reliable—one that gives consistent results—should not be regarded as an intelligence test unless it measures responses which relate to other indices of intellectual functioning. Since there was no "Bureau of Standards" for intellectual measures, the best that Binet could do was to see how the test scores related to teachers' judgments of intelligence. As imperfect as this criterion of validity may seem, it turned out to be adequate for the purpose. Gradually Binet abandoned the attempt to develop tests which theoretically *should* measure intelligence in favor of tests providing measures which correlated with academic ability and in which children's performance improved with age.

In 1904 the French Minister of Public Education appointed a commission to recommend procedures for identifying children who would be unable to profit from regular schools. To aid the commission Binet and Simon developed a test which is the direct ancestor of most modern intelligence tests. It is important to note that the purpose of the test was practical, not theoretical. The sole function of this test was to identify children who were likely to fail in the current school system. Binet made quite clear [Tuddenham, 1962, p. 483] :

**109**

Our goal is not at all to study, to analyze and to disclose the aptitudes of those who are inferior in intelligence. That will be the object of future work. Here we confine ourselves to evaluating, to measuring their intelligence in general; we shall establish their intellectual level; and to give an idea of this level, we shall compare it to normal children of the same age or of an analogous level.

The Binet-Simon test consisted of a series of subtests, each with items of increasing difficulty. The items were so selected that the likelihood of giving a correct answer increased with age. Thus the performance of retarded children could be compared with normal children of the same age. Many types of tests were found useful—naming objects in a picture, repeating a series of digits (digit span), and defining words. Binet's contributions to the study of intelligence were, in a basic sense, both the first and the last. All subsequent intelligence tests were highly influenced by his work, and his tests became the standard against which all other tests were validated or compared.

The Binet tests were improved and revised by Binet as well as others. The Stanford-Binet test, developed by Terman at Stanford University [Terman, 1916; Terman and Merrill, 1937; 1960] yielded the *intelligence quotient*, or IQ, a term with which we are all familiar. The formula used to compute an IQ on this type of test is

$$\frac{\text{Mental age}}{\text{Chronological age}} \times 100$$

where mental age is computed on the basis of the overall test score. A mental age of 10, for example, indicates that overall performance is comparable to that of the average ten-year-old. If a child's mental age equals his chronological age, his IQ is 100. You might compute IQs for two ten-year-old children: one with a mental age of 12, and the other with a mental age of 8.

The original Stanford-Binet test was limited to children, since mental age, as measured from the particular test items used, does not continue to develop greatly after the age of sixteen or so. Since this is the case, the use of the IQ formula with individuals older than sixteen would produce a rapid and unappreciated decline in IQ with age; at age thirty-two the calculated IQ of a normal adult would be 50. To overcome this problem other tests were developed, such as the Wechsler scale [Wechsler, 1958], in which IQ is computed on the basis of how far an individual's test score is above or below the average for others of the same age. In general the two types of tests are based on similar items, and the resulting IQ scores tend to be highly similar.

The tests were so constructed that with 100 as an average IQ the distribution of IQs would approximate a normal curve. **Figure 4-2** shows a theoretical IQ distribution that closely approximates actual test results. As you can see, 50 percent of all IQs range between 90 and 110; only 2.5 percent are above 130 and 2.5 percent are below 70. Note that IQ is not some absolute measure of a physical attribute; it is merely a

**110**

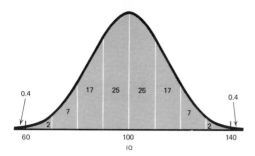

FIGURE 4-2    *A theoretical normal distribution of IQ scores. The percentages shown are the theoretical percentages of the IQ test scores in each 10-point IQ range. These values are very close to the actual percentages in the population except at the extremes (below 70 and above 130).*

measure of an individual's performance on a test in relation to the performances of others of the same age. Obviously an IQ of 100 does not mean that such a person is twice as intelligent as one with an IQ of 50. An IQ of 100 is a score that is equaled or exceeded by 50 percent of the individuals tested, while an IQ of 50 is equaled or exceeded by over 99 percent of the population.

Since most research on intelligence is based on data obtained with some kind of IQ test, it is extremely important to bear in mind how such tests were developed. Their original purpose was to predict academic failure, and the initial criterion of intelligence was teachers' evaluations of children's academic achievement. As a result, the tests include many items which depend on specific knowledge, such as vocabulary. The tests were developed strictly on an empirical basis, and not on the basis of theoretical concepts of intelligence.

In recent years the terms "IQ" and "intelligence" are often used almost interchangeably. This is an unfortunate practice. For example, most of the controversies concerning human "intelligence" are based *solely* on studies of IQ scores. This is legitimate only if it is agreed that intelligence is to be defined as IQ. Furthermore, many questions about the development of intelligence have been studied in infrahumans, but there is no standardized test of infrahuman intelligence. Generally such studies have used some measure of learning ability, but it is not at all clear that learning in infrahumans can be directly related to IQ in humans. An IQ test is not simply a test of learning ability, and tests of infrahuman learning ability do not provide any simple measure of "infrahuman IQ." Thus the evidence from animal studies should be considered with appropriate caution.

Since the first intelligence test was developed there have been several important and controversial questions about the nature of intelligence. Is it something that is learned, or is it inherited? Is the intelligence of an individual stable, or does it vary? Do intelligence tests measure some general ability, or do they measure more than one type of ability? Finally, what are the neurobiological bases of intelligent behavior? We do not yet have final answers to any of these questions.

**111**

## BIOLOGICAL INFLUENCES

Since behavior, whether it is intelligent or stupid, is controlled by the brain, it stands to reason that intelligent behavior must require a good brain. Unfortunately we do not yet know what a "good brain" is. We do, however, know a great deal about bad brains—those that are diseased and injured—and we know a great deal about biological influences on brain function and on certain types of intelligent behavior.

### BRAIN SIZE AND STRUCTURE

In comparison with the brains of most other animals, man's brain is rather large. The average human brain weighs approximately 1300 grams. There are, however, species with larger brains. A dolphin's brain, for example, weighs over 1400 grams [Ridgway et al. 1966]. Obviously brain size alone cannot account for the difference in intellect. A slightly more encouraging observation, at least from man's perspective, is that in man the ratio of brain weight to body weight is approximately 1:45; in the rhinoceros it is 1:3000 and in the whale approximately 1:10,000. However, even the ratio of brain to body weight does not explain man's intellect. As Tobias notes [1970, p. 7]:

. . . it is sobering to see that while Man's exalted brain constitutes just over 2% of his body weight, this percentage is surpassed by the lowly house mouse (2.5% or 1:40), the porpoise with 1:38, the marmoset with 1:19, and the attractive squirrel monkey of tropical America whose brain occupies 1/12 or 8.5% of its body weight.

Of course the human brain differs from those of other animals in structure and organization. One important difference is the amount of brain cortex that is not devoted to specific sensory and motor functions [Hebb, 1949]. Since association cortex is apparently not committed for sensory-motor coordination, it might be involved in higher-level cognitive processes such as learning, thinking, and problem solving. Association cortex constitutes a high proportion of the brain cortex of man. According to this view, for which there is some empirical support, the absolute size of the brain is less important than the ratio of association cortex to cortex with specific sensory-motor functions. It is too early to say whether this particular measure will differentiate the brain of man from brains of other animals in so far as intelligence is concerned. No doubt some distinguishing measure will eventually be found [Tobias, 1970, p. 7]:

Because man, the sapient, did not come out on top [in brain weight or ratio of brain to body weight] it is not surprising that man, the vainglorious and the arrogant, has been searching ever since for an index which would place him unequivocally and unassailably on the highest branch of the tree of life.

One final point about gross brain size deserves mention. Comparison of the brain weights of great men indicate that brain size alone is no key to greatness. While it is true that Oliver Cromwell and Lord Byron had large brains (about 2200 grams), the brain of the great French writer Anatole France weighed only a little over 1000 grams. In view of this, it appears extremely unlikely that variations in gross brain size among men can account for individual differences in intellectual functioning. This does not mean that the brains of great men do not differ from those of ordinary men; it only means that we do not yet know how they differ.

## INBORN ERRORS OF METABOLISM

One of the most obvious facts of brain function is that intellectual functioning can be impaired by disease and injury which affect the brain. Severe impairment of intelligence often results, for example, from diseases such as encephalitis, in which brain cells are damaged by excessive body temperature. Intellectual impairment can also result from numerous hereditary disorders such as phenylketonuria, which is an inherited deficiency in the ability to metabolize phenylalanine. This disorder causes brain damage which results in mental retardation. Severe mental retardation can be prevented, at least reduced, in part, by decreasing the amount of phenylalanine in the diet, but the dietary changes must be introduced in infancy. If phenylketonuric infants are not diagnosed and put on a special diet early in life, permanent mental retardation is highly probable [Woolf et al., 1958].

Harlow found that monkeys reared from birth on a diet high in phenylalanine developed profound and lasting mental retardation [Waisman and Harlow, 1965]. The effects on monkeys given phenylalanine in adolescence were less severe. The excessive phenylalanine appears to produce mental retardation only during infancy, or perhaps early childhood. This finding is consistent with the evidence in children that the earlier the diagnosis and onset of treatment, the greater the likelihood that intellectual performance will not be severely impaired [Berman et al., 1961]. It is interesting to note that although hundreds of monkeys have been tested in the Primate Laboratories of the University of Wisconsin, there has never been an idiot monkey, except, of course, for the experimental animals just described [Harlow and Griffin, 1965]. Apparently, in Harlow's words, "we have to be human to be an inborn idiot." Phenylketonuria is but one of several inborn errors of metabolism known to affect mental functioning.

## NUTRITIONAL FACTORS

There is growing evidence that mental retardation can be caused by inadequate nutrition in infancy. One of the most severe, persistent, and increasing problems of our planet is the inadequate production and unequal distribution of food among its inhabitants. In many areas of the

**113**

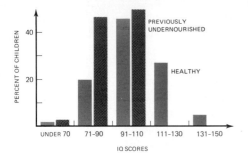

FIGURE 4-3 *Distributions of IQ test scores of normal children and 36 children at ages seven to fourteen who suffered from malnutrition at some time between the ages of four and twenty-four months. None of the malnourished children scored above 110. In comparison with the normal children, a greater percentage had scores of 90 or lower. [Cabak and Najdanovic, 1965]*

world human beings regularly starve to death, while millions of others, particularly children, barely subsist on diets that are inadequate in either calories or protein. The acute symptoms of starvation are, unfortunately, well known because of the publicity given to the relatively frequent outbreaks of famine in underdeveloped regions of the world. What has come to light only in recent years is that acute starvation, such as that seen in the illness *kwashiorkor*, has lasting effects on mental functioning [Eichenwald and Fry, 1969]. *Kwashiorkor* is commonly seen in children whose diet is grossly deficient in protein. Afflicted children become apathetic and sluggish, and without adequate treatment they may, and often do, die.

An even milder degree of malnutrition can cause mental retardation if it occurs in infancy or early childhood. Cabak and Najdanovic, [1965] studied the IQs of a group of seven- to fourteen-year-old Yugoslavian children who had been hospitalized for malnutrition when they were under two years of age. Although the children were underweight by at least 25 percent, the degree of malnutrition was less than that seen in cases of *kwashiorkor*. As Fig. 4-3 shows, the IQs of the undernourished children were clearly lower than those of normal children; none of them had IQs greater than 110. We do not yet have any clear understanding of how undernutrition produces mental retardation. Presumably it is because the lack of adequate protein interferes with normal brain development. However, these findings on the effects of nutrition level on IQ indicate that millions of children throughout the world are, at this moment, becoming mentally retarded simply because of insufficient food. Even worse, these same children are also more likely to suffer from diseases, injuries, and social-deprivation conditions which prevent normal mental development.

## HEREDITARY FACTORS

There is very strong evidence that "normal" variations in intelligence, as well as the more severe disorders such as phenylketonuria, are subject to hereditary influences. Intelligence is not inherited like money from a rich uncle, but IQ scores are strongly influenced by heredity. There are close family resemblances in IQ scores, and in general the closer the relationship—that is, the greater the genetic similarity—the greater the

**114**

similarity in IQ scores. **Figure 4-4** summarizes the results of a number of studies of this relationship. Each point in the figure represents a correlation coefficient obtained in a single study involving a number of pairs of individuals. A correlation coefficient expresses the degree of relationship between two sets of scores. In 14 independent studies of identical twins reared together the correlations ranged from approximately +.75 to +.93—that is, the IQs of each pair of twins were highly similar. By contrast, in four studies the correlations between pairs of unrelated individuals reared together were only about +.15 to +.32. In general, then, the correlation in IQ increases with the degree of genetic relationship. Note also, however, that for all degrees of genetic relationship the correlation is higher if the pairs of individuals are reared together—that is, if their environments are similar. Moreover, the specific correlation coefficients vary greatly from study to study.

What do these correlations indicate? The answer to this question is complex. To begin with IQ is not an attribute; it is a test score. In groups of individuals IQ test scores show a high degree of *heritability*. Heritability is measured as the proportion of the *total* variation of the scores of population (or group of individuals) which is due to genetic factors. If all the measured variation in IQ scores were due to genetic factors, heritability would be 1.00; if all the variation were due to nongenetic factors, heritability would be .00. Of course, since both genetic and environmental influences contribute to the variability of IQ scores, heritability of IQ falls between these two values.

On the basis of the kinds of results shown in **Fig. 4-4** estimates of heritability of IQ have generally ranged around a value of 0.75. That is, for the groups studied, approximately 75 percent of the variation in

FIGURE 4-4    *Genetics, environment, and intelligence. A summary of correlation coefficients obtained in 52 studies of the relationship in IQ between pairs of individuals with varying degrees of genetic relationship. Each point represents the correlation coefficient obtained in a single study. The vertical lines indicate the average (median) coefficient for that particular condition. With the exception of the correlations for unrelated persons living apart, all conditions show positive relationships. The correlations increase with the similarity in genetic makeup and environmental experiences. [Erlenmeyer-Kimling and Jarvik, 1963]*

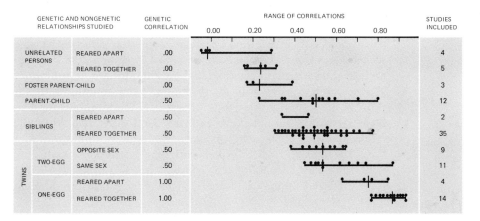

test scores is estimated to be due to genetic factors. This estimate does *not* mean that 75 percent of *any particular individual's* IQ is determined by genetic factors. Heritability refers to groups of individuals, not to single individuals. Moreover, conclusions about heritability are restricted to the particular conditions under which the estimates were obtained. There can be no "true" measure of heritability [Huntley, 1966, p. 201]:

We cannot measure *the* heritability of intelligence once and for all. All that can be offered is an estimate of the heritability of intelligence as measured from scores obtained on a particular test by a particular group of people living at a particular time in a particular area. If any one of these were different the heritability might be different too.

Heritability estimates are strongly influenced by nongenetic influences. In particular, heritability will be high when nongenetic influences are similar for all of the individuals tested. If all individuals in our society were subjected to *identical* nongenetic influences, such as nutrition, disease, injury, and environmental stimulation, then heritability of IQ would be 1.00—that is, all variations in IQ scores could be due only to genetic variation. However, all men are created unequal; genetics guarantees variability, and no society yet has had the ability to create equal nongenetic influences. Even if nongenetic factors were identical, their effects would depend on the genetic makeup of the particular group of individuals tested. Equal exposure to the sun does not produce the same effects on blondes as on brunettes, and normal amounts of phenylalanine in the diet do not have the same effects in normal children as in children who have inherited an inability to metabolize this amino acid. Similarly, the effects on IQ of such nongenetic factors as nutrition and environmental stimulation also vary with genetic makeup. Thus it should be clear that the IQ of an individual is not fixed, or completely determined, by genetic factors. As Hirsch [1970] has pointed out, the fact that heritability estimates of IQ tend to be fairly high does not mean that IQ scores cannot be altered by many nongenetic factors.

In some classical experiments Tryon [1942] demonstrated that rats could be selectively bred for maze-learning ability. Rats obtained from a number of laboratories were trained on a complex maze. Males which made low error scores were mated with comparable females and males which made high scores were mated with high scoring females. The offspring of these initially selected groups of "bright" and "dull" parents did not differ. However, there were clear effects when the selective-breeding procedures were continued for eight generations. Figure 4-5 shows the performance of the parental stock and of generations 1, 3, 6, and 8. Separation of the scores of the two groups was seen as early as the second generation, but complete, or at least almost complete, separation did not occur until the eighth generation. The same results have been obtained in subsequent studies.

The animals in these experiments were reared under fairly constant laboratory conditions. It would be interesting to know whether genetic selection for the maze learning would occur as readily if different

**116**

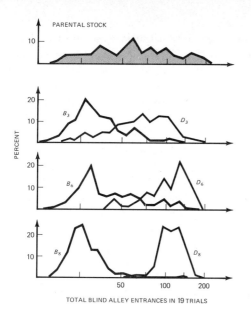

FIGURE 4-5    *Genetic selection for maze-learning performance in rats. The figures show the distribution error scores (blind-alley entrances) of the parental stock of 142 animals and the performances of the third, sixth, and eighth generations of strains selectively bred for maze brightness and maze dullness. The strains were almost completely separated by the eighth generation. [Tryon, 1942]*

animals in each generation were reared under different and changing nutritional and environmental conditions. In all probability selection would be difficult. Subsequent studies of the offspring of the two strains developed by Tryon have shown that the strains did not differ in general learning ability. The maze-bright strains were not uniformly superior to the maze-dull strains on other learning tasks. We do not know why the two genetically different groups of rats differed in maze learning. It could be because of genetic influences on neurobiological processes underlying learning, but the differences could also have resulted from other factors, such as motivation [Searle, 1949]. The same cautions apply to interpretations of the differences in learning of different inbred strains of rats and mice.

# ENVIRONMENTAL INFLUENCES

Environmental influences begin, of course, long before birth. Factors in the intrauterine environment, such as nutrition of the developing organism, undoubtedly influence intelligence. There are many kinds of postnatal environmental influences on behavior. Over 50 years ago the German psychologist Köhler spent several years studying the behavior of chimpanzees on the Tenerife Islands, off the coast of Africa. In his book *The Mentality of Apes* [1925] he described in detail numerous examples of highly intelligent behavior that he witnessed. The apes were not only able to use sticks, but assembled several sticks into a long pole in order to reach bananas that were beyond their reach. Some of the apes were even able to stack boxes in order to reach bananas suspended above them. Köhler stressed that the problems were often solved extremely rapidly, as though the animals had flashes of "insight." The animals he studied were captured in the jungle. Conse-

**117**

quently we do not know the extent to which their rather amazing ability was influenced by previous learning. Subsequent studies of problem solving in monkeys, chimpanzees, and children have shown that this type of behavior is exhibited only after extensive problem-solving experience. Flashes of natural insight are not made by untutored brains.

In an extensive series of studies Harlow [1949b] has shown that, with training, monkeys can learn to learn. Their ability to solve complex discrimination problems can be dramatically improved by intensive training on a variety of simple and complex problems. Although the ability to solve complex problems is undoubtedly influenced by genetic factors, obviously such intelligent behavior in monkeys is also highly modifiable by experience. Learning to learn is no doubt an essential feature of the intellectual development of monkeys, apes, and children growing up in their natural environments.

Since the development of the first IQ test there has been considerable disagreement concerning the effect of experience on IQ [Jensen, 1969]. The extreme view that IQ scores provide a pure measure of inherited intelligence is not widely held by psychologists. In fact IQ tests are more often criticized because they do not measure intellectual ability which is independent of experience. Binet's position on this controversial issue was clear; he was convinced that intelligence, as measured by his test, could be improved by training [in Tuddenham, 1962, p. 488]:

Having on our hands children who did not know how to listen, to pay attention, to keep quiet we pictured our first duty as being not to teach them the facts that we thought would be most useful, but *to teach them how to learn*. We have therefore devised . . . what we call exercizes in mental orthopedics [practice in sitting still, carrying a full glass, etc.]. . . . In the same way that physical orthopedics straightens a crooked spine, mental orthopedics strengthens, cultivates, and fortifies attention, memory, perception, [and] judgment. . . . With practice . . . one can succeed in . . . becoming literally more intelligent than before.

Does IQ remain constant, or is it like the ability to learn to learn, influenced by experience? The evidence that intelligence is influenced by heredity does not require the assumption that it is unvarying. Height is highly influenced by heredity, but one's absolute height as well as one's height in relation to others changes with age. There is quite clear evidence that IQ scores of individuals may vary considerably over time. One reason is that the types of questions included in IQ tests are different for different ages. Obviously the questions that can be asked of two-year-old children are different from those that can be asked of older children, as well as from those which are appropriate for adults. IQ test scores can also be depressed by temporary conditions such as illness or emotional states. The intellectual abilities of individuals may be improved by experience.

Studies of IQ test scores of individuals tested several times over a period of years indicate that the greater the time interval between the

| CHANGES IN IQ | NO. OF CHILDREN | PERCENT |
| --- | --- | --- |
| Less than 9 points | 33 | 15 |
| More than 10 points | 189 | 85 |
| More than 15 points | 129 | 58 |
| More than 20 points | 78 | 35 |
| More than 30 points | 20 | 9 |
| More than 50 points | 1 | 0.5 |

TABLE 4-1    *Changes in IQ from ages six to eighteen [Honzik et. al., 1948].*

tests, the less the similarity in the IQ scores. Table 4-1 shows the findings of a study of IQ changes in children tested eight times between the ages of six and eighteen. Only 15 percent of those tested showed changes of less than 9 points; over 35 percent of the differences in IQ score were greater than 20 points. In one case a child's IQ fluctuated from 128 to 113 to 163 to 111, depending on whether the tests were administered during stable periods of his life or during periods of disturbing home influences [Honzik et al., 1948]. Significant increases in IQ have been found in individuals who had moved to an environment that provided better education and increased social stimulation. The IQs of blacks reared in the South have been shown to increase when they move to northern cities. Studies of children brought up in a kibbutz in Israel, where they are given nursery school rearing for 22 hours a day for four years or more, suggest that this experience increases the children's IQ scores. The average IQs of kibbutz-reared children is 115, in comparison with IQs of 85 and 105, respectively, for mid-Eastern and European Jewish children brought up in individual homes [Bloom, 1969].

At least part of the differences in IQ scores obtained in different regions of the world are due to cultural differences in the responses to the questions on the test. Tests developed to measure the performance of urban European or American school children may or may not be appropriate for children in other cultural settings. One somewhat extreme example of the responses of a child from a rural area illustrates this problem [Pressey, in Klineberg, 1969, pp. 69–70]:

[The tester] presented the familiar Binet problem: "If you went to the store and bought six cents worth of candy and gave the clerk ten cents, what change would you receive?" One youngster replied, "I never had ten cents and if I did I wouldn't spend it for candy, and anyway candy is what your mother makes." The examiner made a second attempt and reformulated his question as follows: "If you had taken ten cows to pasture for your father and six of them strayed away, how many would you have left to drive home?" The child replied, "We don't have ten cows but if we did, and I lost six, I wouldn't dare go home." The examiner made one last attempt: "If there were ten children in a school and six of them came out with the measles, how many would there be in school?" The answer came even more promptly: "None, because the rest would be afraid of catching it too."

This example also illustrates another general and important point about IQ tests. The tests require answers which can only have been learned. To be sure, they require *more* than retention of previously learned information, but the fact that such information is assumed should not be overlooked. An answer to the problem presented in the example above requires an elementary knowledge of arithmetic as well as the ability to reason. The vocabulary test, which is included in most intelligence tests, is an even better example. The answer to the question, "What is an apple?" is not supplied by one's genes. IQ tests are based on a general assumption that most individuals tested will have been exposed to the information requested. It is not certain that all children, even in the affluent United States, will know about apples. The answer to a question on one intelligence test requires the knowledge that moss grows on the north side of trees. Where does moss grow in the deserts of Arizona, Nevada, and New Mexico? Television does not solve this problem for children reared in the deserts of Africa. A more obvious problem is the use of IQ tests in English with children from homes in which English is not spoken. This practice is still common in many parts of the United States, and no doubt provides empirical support for the view that certain ethnic groups tend to have low IQs.

A number of studies have reported slightly lower average IQs in groups of blacks than in groups of whites in the United States. Some investigators have inferred that these average differences in IQ are due to genetic differences. Several factors, however, render any such inference invalid. To begin with, blacks in the United States have not had, and do not have, environments which are similar to those of whites. As in any group isolated from the mainstream of society, there are many cultural, linguistic, and experiential differences. In addition, there are differences in the incidence of disease, the quality of nutrition, and the quality of education. When the environmental differences are decreased, the differences in tested IQs of blacks and whites tend to decrease. In a study of draftee scores on the Army Alpha test during World War I it was found that in all states the average scores of blacks were lower than those of whites. However, the average scores for blacks in several northern states were higher than those for whites in several southern states [Yerkes, 1921]. Furthermore, for both whites and blacks, the average IQ of the draftees from each state varied directly with the state's average expenditure for public education; for both blacks and whites the correlation between average IQ and average expenditure of the state for education was approximately +.70 [Spuhler and Lindzey, 1967].

Since expenditures for education have great bearing on the quality of education, it appears that IQ is influenced by educational experiences. Of course there is probably also a correlation between expenditures for public education and expenditures for public health. Thus the cause of the correlation between expenditures for education and IQ of the recruits from each state is not a simple matter. Regardless of the reasons, it is clear that the IQs of blacks and whites alike are influenced by environmental factors. In fact, as Washburn comments [1963, p. 529]:

I am sometimes surprised to hear it stated that if Negroes were given an equal opportunity, their I.Q. would be the same as the Whites. If one looks at the degree of social discrimination against Negroes and their lack of education, and also takes into account the tremendous amount of overlapping between I.Q.'s of both, one can make an equally good case that, given a comparable chance to that of Whites, their I.Q.'s would test out ahead. Of course, it would be absolutely unimportant in a democratic society if this were to be true, because the vast majority of individuals of both groups would be of comparable intelligence.

## INTELLIGENCE AND ACHIEVEMENT

As we have seen, IQ test scores can be profoundly influenced by culture. Nevertheless, the biological contributions to intelligence, such as genetics, nutrition, and disease, indicate that some aspects of intelligence depend more on having a "good brain" than they do on cultural experiences. Recent studies by Cattell [1968] indicate that intelligence tests may well measure two different types of intelligence. *Fluid intelligence*, according to Cattell, is fairly free from cultural influence and appears to be fairly closely related to overall physiological efficiency. This type of intelligence increases up to the age of about twenty and then gradually declines. Fluid intelligence appears to be roughly a measure of judgment and reasoning. *Crystallized intelligence* is seen in skills that are influenced by experience, such as vocabulary, mechanical knowledge, and in general, knowledge of facts and skills. As might be expected, crystallized intelligence increases steadily with age because of increased opportunity for acquiring knowledge and skills. For example, Cattell reports that he has studied [1968, p. 58]:

> . . . deck hands and farmers who scored [quite high] in fluid ability but who acquired no comparable level of crystallized ability because they had not systematically applied their fluid intelligence to what is usually called culture. Such men will astonish you in a game of chess or by solving a wire puzzle with which you have struggled in vain, or in swift insights into men and their motives. But their vocabularies may be arrested at a colloquial level, their knowledge of history negligible, and they may never have encountered algebra or geometry.

It is too early to tell whether this simplified view of intelligence is valid. If it is, it should help clarify some of the controversial issues which surround the general problem of human intelligence. It may be possible, as Cattell has suggested, to develop tests that provide relatively pure measures of fluid intelligence, tests which are minimally influenced by cultural differences, but this possibility seems remote. As we have seen, intelligent behavior results from a large number of influences on brain development and function. Intelligence is not simply the functioning of the nervous system with culture "added on."

The complex way in which biological factors interact with experience in influencing later abilities is seen in studies of the effects of environmental stimulation on learning ability in rats. Several studies have shown that rats reared in a complex environment are better in maze learning than rats reared in a conventional laboratory cage. Studies by Bennett et al. [1964] show that the brains of environmentally "enriched" rats are different in a number of ways from those of either normal or environmentally deprived rats, indicating that the general environmental stimulation appears to have biological as well as psychological effects. Other research has shown that the maze-learning ability of rats reared in an enriched environment can be improved by giving the young rats daily injections of drugs which stimulate the central nervous system. Their learning ability is improved even if the drug and environmental stimulation treatments are administered only when the rats are young and the learning tests are not given until several weeks after the last drug treatment [LeBoeuf and Peeke, 1969; Shandro and Shaeffer, 1969]. These conditions suggest that the drug appears to produce rather permanent improvement in the ability to learn. We do not yet know the basis of the facilitation. We do not know whether the conditions of these experiments produce a general improvement in learning ability for tasks other than mazes. It is interesting to note that the same drug injections result in *impaired* learning ability if the rats are reared in an environment which offers little stimulation. The drug cannot offset the effects of impoverished environmental stimulation. It is obvious that biological and psychological factors interact in complex ways to produce what is measured either as IQ in human beings or learning ability in infrahumans.

## THE IDIOT SAVANT: AN UNSOLVED PROBLEM

We all vary in our special talents as well as in our intelligence, but in general our abilities in special areas are not grossly different from our general intellectual abilities. The *idiot savant* is a striking exception. This dramatic and puzzling phenomenon is best defined by example. Horwitz et al., [1965] described a pair of identical twins with IQs of approximately 60 to 70, well below normal, but with uncanny memories for dates. Furthermore, they were "calendar calculators"; they were able to give almost instantaneously the day of the week for any date over a range of centuries. One twin had a range of at least 6000 years. When asked the years in which a given date, such as April 21, would fall on a Sunday, both twins correctly answered 1968, 1957, 1946, etc. One twin, when encouraged, continued to give the correct years as far back as 1700. The twins were also able to reply that the fourth Monday in February, 1993, will be the twenty-second or that the third Monday in May, 1936, was the eighteenth. The ability to perform these calculations is all the more impressive in view of the fact that neither twin was able to add, subtract, multiply, or divide numbers, even single digits. Thus, although they were unable to add up to 30, when told a person's birth date, they were able to tell that it would be 30 weeks until the person's next birthday or 13 weeks since he last had a birthday.

An examination of the histories of these twins has revealed nothing that suggests an explanation. The only fact of any significance is that the twin who was best at calendar calculating discovered a perpetual calendar in an almanac when he was six and spent hours poring over it. The other twin developed an interest in the calendar several years later. However, the availability of the calendar and the expression of interest in it does not explain their ability to calculate. This is a very special, unique talent found in two otherwise mentally retarded boys. When the twins were asked how they were able to perform the calculations, they could only respond, "It's in my head." With our present knowledge we cannot actually do much better. As Holstein notes [1965, p. 1078] :

> The importance . . . of the Idiot-Savant lies in our inability to explain him; he stands as a landmark of our own ignorance and the phenomenon of the Idiot-Savant exists as a challenge to our capabilities.

The problem of the *idiot savant* is part of the much larger question of the psychobiological bases of intelligence. Since we do not yet understand the bases of normal variations in intelligence, the *idiot savant* presents no greater mystery. It merely serves to remind us of our present ignorance of how intelligent behavior is controlled by the machinery of the brain.

## IQ AS A PREDICTOR OF ACHIEVEMENT

The *idiot savant* achieves "distinction" in one highly special area, but this talent, regardless of its degree, does not provide a basis for his adaptation to a complex environment. In the most fundamental sense intelligent behavior is adaptive. IQ tests were originally developed to predict the ability of children to perform in school—that is, their ability to adapt to the requirements of the classroom. To a great extent they have succeeded in this. All in all the IQ score remains the best predictor of scholastic success. In numerous studies of the relationship between IQ scores and college grade-point average, for example, the correlations have averaged slightly better than +.50. Clearly this is not perfect correlation. However, IQ could not be expected to provide a perfect prediction of scholastic success since so many factors contribute to academic performance—illness, emotional problems, distractions, motivation, study habits, and just plain hard work. Application, including application of the seat of the pants to the seat of the chair, is a necessary condition even though it is not a sufficient condition.

The IQ test, then, is an effective predictor of academic performance, but does it predict anything else? Do individuals with high IQ scores tend to do better outside of school? The answer is, quite clearly, yes. Individuals with high IQs are often referred to as "gifted," and no doubt they are. They have received adequate nutrition and stimulating environments, and they have been protected from injury to their brains. In this sense they are indeed gifted—but the gift is not solely genetic, as has often been implied.

In 1921 Terman, who developed the Stanford-Binet intelligence test, began a long-term study of 1500 children with IQ scores of 140 or higher. At that time the children were eleven years old. The study examined in some detail the physical characteristics, behavior, and accomplishments of most of the subjects over half a century. These gifted individuals are still being studied by Terman's colleagues, and a complete report will not be forthcoming perhaps until after the turn of the century [Terman, 1925; Terman and Oden, 1947; 1959]. However, there have been a number of important and interesting findings thus far [Butcher, 1968].

The results of this study do not support the popular view that IQ compensates for deficiencies in physical ability, health, or personality. In comparison with average children, the gifted children were heavier at birth, learned to walk earlier, talked earlier, and matured physically at an earlier age. They did not differ significantly from average children in sociability, masculinity or femininity, popularity, or social maladjustment. Moreover, they performed well both inside and outside of school. Their school performance was highly accelerated (about 40 percent faster than average), and they performed, on the average, at a level of the top 10 percent in high school. More than 90 percent of the boys and 80 percent of the girls went to college. The average income of the group has been quite high, and the literary and scientific achievement has been most impressive. As of 1959 the group had to its credit 33 novels, many hundreds of shorter writings, 230 patents, and about 2000 scientific papers. Clearly these individuals are richly talented. It is worth noting, however, that the study did not reveal an Albert Einstein, a Leonardo da Vinci, a Thomas Edison, or a George Washington Carver. Such individuals appear much less frequently than 1 in 1500—even in 1500 gifted.

Overall, Terman's study has provided extensive evidence that the IQ test predicts more than performance in primary school. Of course intellectual ability is no guarantee of success, even in intellectual areas of achievement. Not all the gifted children achieved distinction—and, no doubt, equal or greater distinction has been achieved by many children who were not included in the studies because their IQ scores were below 140. High IQ is associated with high levels of achievement in a wide variety of tasks and occupations, but it does not account for all the variation in performance; at best, it accounts for only about half. There is plenty of room for such factors as motivation.

Terman's study of gifted individuals is only a descriptive study. It provides no additional specific clues to the bases of intelligence. Presumably the gifted have "good brains," but we do not yet know how to distinguish the brain of a gifted child from that of an *idiot savant*.

The nature and bases of intelligence are obviously extremely complex. Intelligent behavior is at least the outcome, and yet more than the outcome, of the efficient functioning of all the basic processes underlying sensory-motor integration, learning, and memory. We are only beginning to understand the factors that contribute to individual and species differences in intelligence. The problems of the bases of intelligence constitute some of the major unsolved problems of science.

## SUMMARY

Intelligence is, in its most basic sense, synonymous with intelligent behavior. Thus intelligence is exhibited by many animals, and man's superior intelligence seems to be related to his position on the phylogenetic scale rather than to any qualitative difference between "reason" and "instinct." The basis of this superiority is not yet clear, but of the many factors that have been explored, such as gross brain size and ratio of brain weight to body weight, the most significant difference is in the relative amount of association area in the sensory cortex of the brain. The most outstanding contribution to the study of human intelligence was the first useful intelligence test, developed by Binet on a completely empirical basis as a predictor of academic ability. The later Stanford-Binet test yields the familiar IQ score, which unfortunately has come to be used interchangeably with "intelligence."

The development of intelligence is markedly affected by such factors as injury, disease, inborn errors of metabolism, and malnutrition. Genetic studies indicate that intelligence is also influenced to a great extent by heredity. There is considerable controversy over environmental influences, chiefly because all studies are based on comparison of IQ scores. It is clear, however, that cultural, educational, and social variables are important factors in measured IQ. The interaction of biological and environmental variables also plays a major role, especially in relation to learning ability in animals. For example, in rats an enriched environment apparently increases learning ability, causes discernible differences in neural anatomy, and determines the effect of drug injections on learning ability. However, we still know very little about the neural bases of intelligence. The classical case of the *idiot savant* is merely one of the unsolved problems, and although IQ is an effective predictor of future overall achievement, it tells us nothing about the actual nature of human intelligence.

# BIBLIOGRAPHY

Adair, L., Wilson, J. E., Zemp, J., and Glassman, E. 1968. Brain function and macromolecules. III. Uridine incorporated into polysomes of mouse brain during short-term avoidance conditioning. *Proc. Nat. Acad. Sci.*, 61, 606–613.

Agranoff, B. W. 1968. Biological effects of antimetabolites used in behavioral studies. In D. H. Efron et al. (Eds.), *Psychopharmacology: A review of progress.* PHS Publ. No. 1836, 909–917. Washington, D.C.: U. S. Government Printing Office.

Alpern, H. P. 1968. Facilitation of learning by implantation of strychnine sulphate in the central nervous system. (Doctoral dissertation, University of California) Irvine, Calif.

Applewhite, P.B. 1968. Nonlocal nature of habituation in a rotifer and protozoan. *Nature*, 217, 287–288.

Baddeley, A.D. 1964. Semantic and acoustic similarity in short-term memory. *Nature*, 204, 1116–1117.

Barbizet, J. 1963. Defect of memorizing of hippocampal-mammillary origin: A review. *J. Neurol. Neurosur. Psych.*, 26, 127–135. (By permission of the Editor, *J. Neurol. Neurosur. Psych.)*

Barondes, S. H. 1968. Effects of inhibitors of cerebral protein synthesis on "long-term" memory in mice. In D. H. Efron et al. (Eds.), *Psychopharmacology: A review of progress.* PHS Publ. No. 1836, 905–908. Washington, D. C.: U. S. Government Printing Office.

Bartlett, F. C. 1932. *Remembering.* London: Cambridge University Press.

Bennett, E. L., Diamond, M. C., Krech, D., and Rosenzweig, M. R. 1964. Chemical and anatomical plasticity of brain. *Science,* 146, 610–619. (Copyright 1964 by the American Association for the Advancement of Science, by permission.)

Berman, P. W., Graham, F. K., Eichman, P. L., and Waisman, H. A. 1961. Psychologic and neurologic status of diet-treated phenylketonuric children and their siblings. *Pediatrics,* 28, 924.

Birch, H. G. 1945. The relation of previous experience to insightful problem solving. *J. Comp. Psychol.*, 38, 367–383.

Bitterman, E. R. 1965. The evolution of intelligence. *Scient. Amer.*, 212, 92–100.

Bliss, J. C., Crane, H. D., Mansfield, P. K., and Townsend, J. 1966. Information available in brief tactile presentations. *Perceptual Psychophysiol.*, 1, 273–283.

Bloom, B. S. 1969. Letter to the editor. *Harvard Educ. Rev.*, 39, 419–421.

Bourne, L. E., Jr. 1966. *Human conceptual behavior.* Boston: Allyn and Bacon. (By permission of the publisher.)

Bovet, D., Bovet-Nitti, F., and Oliverio, A. 1969. Genetic aspects of learning and memory in mice. *Science*, 163, 139–149. (Copyright 1969 by the American Association for the Advancement of Science, by permission.)

Breland, K., and Breland, M. 1961. The misbehavior of organisms. *Amer. Psychol.*, 16, 681–684. (Copyright 1961 by the American Psychological Association, reproduced by permission.)

Brown, R., and Bellugi, U. 1964. Three processes in the child's acquisition of syntax. *Harvard Educ. Rev.*, 34, 133–151.

Brown, R., and McNeill, D. 1966. The "tip of the tongue" phenomenon. *J. Verbal Learn, Verbal Behav.*, 5, 325–337.

Bruce, D. J., Evans, C. R., Fenwick, P. B., and Spencer, V. 1970. Effect of present novel verbal material during slow wave sleep. *Nature*, 225, 873–874.

Bruner, J. S., Goodnow, J. J., and Austin, G. A. 1956. *A study of thinking.* New York: Wiley.

Butcher, H. J. 1968. *Human intelligence: Its nature and assessment.* New York: Barnes and Noble. (By permission.)

Butler, R. A. 1953. Discrimination learning by

rhesus monkeys to visual-exploration motivation. *J. Comp. Physiol. Psychol.* 46, 95–98. (Copyright 1953 by the American Psychological Association, reproduced by permission.)

Butler, R.A. 1954*b*. Curiosity in monkeys. *Scient. Amer.*, 190, 70–75.

Byrne, W. L., (Ed.). 1970. *Molecular approaches to learning and memory.* New York: Academic Press.

Cabak, V., and Najdanovic, R. 1965. Effect of undernutrition in early life on physical and mental development. *Arch. Dis. in Child.*, 40, 532–534. (By permission of the authors and the Editor, *Arch. Dis. in Childhood.*)

Campbell, B. A. 1967. Development studies of learning and motivation in infra-primate mammals. In H. W. Stevenson (Ed.), *Early behavior: Comparative and developmental approaches.* New York: Wiley.

Campbell, B. A., and Pickleman, J. R. 1961. The imprinting object as a reinforcing stimulus. *J. Comp. Physiol. Psychol.*, 54, 592–596.

Cattell, J. M. 1890. Mental tests and measurements. *Mind*, 15, 373–381.

Cattell, R. B. 1968. Are I.Q. tests intelligent? *Psychol. Today*, 2, 56–62. (By permission.)

Cherkin, A. 1969. Kinetics of memory consolidation: Role of amnesic treatment parameters. *Proc. Natl. Acad. Sci.*, 63, 1094–1101.

Chomsky, N. 1957. *Syntactic Structures.* The Hague: Mouton.

Chomsky, N. 1965. *Aspects of the theory of snytax.* Cambridge: MIT Press.

Chomsky, N. 1968. *Language and the mind.* New York: Harcourt, Brace and World.

Conrad, R. 1958. Accuracy of recall using keyset and telephone dial and the effect of a prefix digit. *J. Appl. Psychol.*, 42, 285–288.

Dale, H.C.A. 1964. Retroactive interference in short-term memory. *Nature*, 203, 1408.

Darwin, C. 1859. *The origin of species.* New York: A. L. Fowle, International Science Library.

Darwin, C. 1872. *The expression of the emotions in man and animals.* New York: D. Appleton. Reprinted in 1965 by University of Chicago Press.

Deese, J. 1970. *Psycholinguistics.* Boston: Allyn and Bacon. (By permission of the publisher.)

Denti, A., McGaugh, J. L., Landfield, P. W., and Shinkman, P. 1970. Further study of the effects of posttrial electrical stimulation of the mesencephalic reticular formation on avoidance learning in rats. *Physiol. Behav.*, 5, 659–662.

Deutsch, J. A. 1969. The physiological basis of memory. *Amer. Rev. Psychol.*, 20, 85–104.

Drachman, D. A., and Arbit, J. 1966. Memory and the hippocampal complex. II. Is memory a multiple process? *Arch. Neurol.*, 15, 52–61. (By permission.)

Duncan, C. P. 1949. The retroactive effects of electroshock on learning. *J. Comp. Physiol. Psychol.*, 42, 32–34.

Ebbinghaus, H. 1885. *Uber das gedachtniss.* Leipzig: Drucker and Humblat.

Eichenwald, H. F., and Fry, P. C. 1969. Nutrition and learning. *Science*, 163, 644–648.

Eisenstein, E. M., and Cohen, M. J. 1965. Learning in an isolated prothoracic insect ganglion. *Animal Behav.*, 13, 104–108. (By permission.)

Erlenmeyer-Kimling, L., and Jarvik, L. F. 1963. Genetics and intelligence: A review. *Science*, 142, 1477–1479. (Copyright 1963 by the American Association for the Advancement of Science, by permission.)

Fishbein, W. 1970. Interference with conversion of memory from short-term to long-term storage by partial sleep deprivation. *Commun. Behav. Biol.*, 5, 171–175.

Fox, B. H., and Robbin, J. S. 1952. The retention of material presented during sleep. *J. Exp. Psychol.*, 43, 75–79.

Freedman, L. Z. 1960. Truth drugs. *Scient. Amer.*, 202, 145–157.

French, G. M., and Harlow, H. F. 1962. Variability of delayed-reaction performance in normal and brain-damaged rhesus monkeys. *J. Neurophysiol.*, 25, 585–599.

Garcia, J., McGowan, B. K., Ervin, F. R., and Koelling, R. A. 1968. Cues: Their relative effectiveness as a function of the reinforcer. *Science*, 160, 794–795. (Copyright 1968 by the American Association for the Advancement of Science, by permission.)

Gardner, B. T., and Gardner, R. A. 1970. Two-way communication with an infant chimpanzee. In A. Schrier and F. Stollnitz (Eds.), *Behavior of nonhuman primates.* New York: Academic, in press. (By permission.)

Gardner, R. A., and Gardner, B. T. 1969. Teaching sign language to a chimpanzee. *Science,* 165, 664–672.

Geller, A., and Jarvik, M. E. 1968. The time relations of ECS induced amnesia. *Psychonomic Sci.,* 12, 169–170.

Gerard, R. W. 1949. Physiology and psychiatry. *Amer. J. Psych.,* 106, 161–173.

Glassman, E. 1969. The biochemistry of learning: An evaluation of the role of RNA and protein. *Amer. Rev. Biochem.,* 38, 605–646.

Gleitman, H. 1970. Forgetting in animals: Phenomena and explanatory theories. In W. K. Honig and P.H.R. James (Eds.), *Animal memory.* New York: Academic Press, in press. (By permission.)

Glickman, S. E. 1961. Perseverative neural processes and consolidation of memory trace. *Psychol. Bull.,* 58, 218–233.

Golub, A. M., Masiarz, F. R., Villars, T., and McConnell, J. V. 1970. Incubation effects in behavior induction in rats. *Science,* 168, 392–395.

Gottlieb, G. 1965. Imprinting in relation to parental and species identification by avian neonates. *J. Comp. Physiol. Psychol.,* 59, 345–356.

Gross, C. G., Bender, D. B., and Rocha-Miranda, C. E. 1969. Visual receptive fields of neurons in inferotemporal cortex of the monkey. *Science,* 166, 1303–1305.

Groves, P. M., and Thompson, R. F. 1970. Habituation: A dual-process theory. *Psychol. Rev.,* 77, 412–450. (Copyright 1970 by the American Psychological Association, reproduced by permission.)

Haber, R. N. 1970. How we remember what we see. *Scient. Amer.,* 222, 104–112.

Haber, R. N., and Haber, R. B. 1964. Eidetic imagery. I. Frequency. *Perceptual Motor Skills,* 19, 131–138.

Haber, R. N., and Standing, L. G. 1969. Direct measures of short-term visual storage. *Quart. J. Exp. Psychol.,* 21, 43–54.

Harlow, H. F. 1949a. The formation of learning sets. *Psychol. Rev.,* 56, 51–56. (Copyright 1949 by the American Psychological Association, reproduced by permission.)

Harlow, H. F. 1949b. The nature of learning sets. *Psychol. Rev.,* 56, 51–65.

Harlow, H. F. 1952. Functional organization of the brain in relation to mentation and behavior. In *The biology of mental health and*

diseases. Ch. 16. New York: Paul B. Hoeber Inc., Medical Book Dept. of Harper and Brothers.

Harlow, H. F. 1959a. The development of learning in the rhesus monkey. *Amer. Sci.,* 47, 459–479. (By permission.)

Harlow, H. F., and Griffin, G. 1965. Induced mental and social deficits in rhesus monkeys. In S. F. Asler and R. E. Cooke (Eds.), *The biosocial basis of mental retardation.* Baltimore: Johns Hopkins Press.

Harlow, H. F., and McClearn, G. E. 1954. Object discrimination learned by monkeys on the basis of manipulation motives. *J. Comp. Physiol. Psychol.,* 47, 73–76.

Hartry, A. L., Keith-Lee, P., and Morton, W. D. 1964. Planaria: Memory transfer through cannibalism re-examined. *Science,* 146, 274–275.

Hayes, C. 1951. *The ape in our house.* New York: Harper.

Hayes, K. J., and Hayes, C. 1951. The intellectual development of a home-raised chimpanzee. *Proc. Ameri. Phil. Soc.,* 95, 105–109.

Hebb, D. O. 1949. *The organization of behavior.* New York: Wiley.

Hebb, D. O. 1958. Alice in Wonderland or psychology among the biological sciences. In H. F. Harlow and C. N. Woolsey (Eds.), *Biological and biochemical bases of behavior.* Madison: University of Wisconsin Press. (Copyright © 1958 by the Regents of the University of Wisconsin, by permission.)

Hebb, D. O. 1961. Distinctive features of learning in the higher animal. In J. F. Delafresnaye et al. (Eds.), *Brain mechanisms and learning.* Oxford, England: Blackwell Scientific Publ. (By permission.)

Hediger, H. 1950. *Wild animals in captivity.* London: Butterworth.

Heidbreder, E. 1946. The attainment of concepts. I. Methodology and terminology. *J. Gen. Psychol.,* 35, 173–189. (By permission.)

Heine, R. 1914. Uber Wiredererkennen und ruckinirkinde Hemmung. *Z. Psychol.,* 68, 161–236.

Heinroth, O., and Heinroth, K. 1959. *The birds.* London: Faber and Faber.

Herbert, M. J. and Harsh, C. M. 1944. Observational learning by cats. *J. Comp. Physiol. Psychol.,* 37, 81–95.

Hess, E. H. 1957. Effects of meprobamate on imprinting in waterfowl. *Ann. New York Acad. Sci.,* 67 (10), 724–733. (Copyright ©

1957 by The New York Academy of Sciences, reprinted by permission.)

Hirsch, J. 1970. Behavior genetic analysis and its biosocial consequences. *Seminars in Psych.*, 2, 89–105.

Holstein, A. P. 1965. Discussion of "identical twins—'idiot savants'—calendar calculators." *Amer. J. Psych.*, 121, 1077–1078. (By permission.)

Honzik, M. P., Macfarlane, J. W., and Allen, L. 1948. The stability of mental test performance between two and eighteen years. *J. Exp. Educ.*, 18, 309–324.

Horridge, G. A. 1965. The electrophysiological approach to learning in the isolatable ganglia. *Animal Behav.*, Suppl. 1, 163–182.

Horwitz, W. A., Kestenbaum, C., Person, E., and Jarvik, L. 1965. Identical twin—"idiot savants"—calendar calculators. *Amer. J. Psych.*, 121, 1075–1079.

Hubel, D. H., and Wiesel, T. N. 1959. Receptive fields of single neurons in the cat's striate cortex. *J. Physiol.*, 148, 574–591.

Hudspeth, W. J., and Wilsoncroft, W. E. 1970. Retrograde amnesia time-dependent effects of rhinencephalic lesions. *J. Neurobiol.*, 1, 221–232.

Hull, C. L. 1943. *Principles of behavior.* New York: Appleton-Century-Crofts.

Hunter, I. 1957. *Memory.* Baltimore: Penguin Books.

Hunter, W. S. 1913. The delayed reaction in animals and children. *Behav. Monogr.*, 2, 1–86.

Huntley, R.M.C. 1966. Heritability of intelligence. In J. E. Meade and A. S. Parkes (Eds.), *Genetic and environmental factors in human ability.* New York: Plenum Press. (By permission.)

Huppert, F. A., and Deutsch, J. A. 1969. Improvement in memory with time. *Quart. J. Exp. Psychol.*, 21, 267–271.

Hyden, H. 1967. RNA in brain cells. In G. C. Quarton, T. Melnechuk, and F. O. Schmitt (Eds.), *The neurosciences.* New York: Rockefeller.

Jacobsen, C. F. 1935. Functions of the frontal association area in primates. *Arch. Neurol. Psych.*, 33, 558–569.

Jacobson, E. 1931. Electrical measurements of neuromuscular states during mental activities. VIII. Imagination, recollection and abstract thinking involving the speech musculature. *Amer. J. Physiol.*, 97, 200–209. (By permission.)

James, H. 1959. Flicker: An unconditioned stimulus for imprinting. *Can. J. Psychol.*, 13, 59–67.

James, W. 1890. *The principles of psychology.* New York: Henry Holt. Reprinted 1950, Vol. I. New York: Dover.

Jarvik, M. E. 1968. The significance of retrograde amnesia (RA) and forgetting in the problem of memory storage. In D. Bovet, F. Bovet-Nitti, and A. Oliverio (Eds.), *Recent advances on learning and retention.* Rome: Roma Accademia Nazionale dei Lincei.

Jenkins, J. G., and Dallenbach, K. M. 1924. Oblivescence during sleep and waking. *Amer. J. Psychol.*, 35, 605–612.

Jensen, A. R. 1969. How much can we boost I.Q. and scholastic achievement? *Harvard Educ. Rev.*, 39, 1–123.

Jensen, D. D. 1965. Paramecia, planaria and pseudo learning. *Animal Behav.*, Suppl. 1, 9–20.

John, E. R. 1967. *Mechanisms of memory.* New York: Academic Press. (By permission.)

Klineberg, O. 1969. *Characteristics of the american negro.* New York: Harper and Row.

Köhler, W. 1925. *The mentality of apes.* New York: Harcourt, Brace.

Konishi, M. 1965. The role of auditory feedback in the control of vocalization in the white-crowned sparrow. *Z. Tierpsychol.*, 22, 770–785.

Konorski, J. 1967. *Integrative activity of the brain.* Chicago: University of Chicago Press.

Koukkou, M., and Lehmann, D. 1968. EEG and memory storage in sleep experiments with humans. *Electroenceph. Clin. Neurophysiol.*, 25, 455–462.

Krivanek, J., and McGaugh, J. L. 1968. Effects of pentylenetetrazol on memory storage in mice. *Psychopharmacologia*, 12, 303–321. (By permission.)

Lashley, K. S. 1951. The problem of serial order in behavior. In L. A. Jeffress (Ed.). *Cerebral mechanisms of behavior.* New York: Wiley.

Lashley, K. S. 1960. In search of the engram. In F. A. Beach, D. O. Hebb, C. T. Morgan, and H. W. Nissen (Eds.), *The neuropsychology of Lashley.* New York: McGraw-Hill.

Lashley, K. S., and McCarthy, D. A. 1926. The survival of the maze habit after cerebellar

injuries. *J. Comp. Physiol. Psychol.*, 6,
423–433.

LeBoeuf, B. J., and Peeke, H.V.S. 1969. The
effect of strychnine administration during
development on adult maze learning in the
rat. *Psychopharmacologia*, 16, 49–53.

Lenneberg, E. H. 1967. *The biological foundations of language.* New York: Wiley. (By
permission.)

Liddell, H. S. 1942. The conditioned reflex.
In F. A. Moss (Ed.), *Comparative psychology.* Englewood Cliffs, N. J.: Prentice-Hall.

Lindauer, M. 1961. *Communication among
social bees.* Cambridge: Harvard University
Press.

Lorenz. K. 1937. The companion in the bird's
world. *Auk*, 54, 245–273.

Lorenz, K. 1957. The nature of instinct. In
C. H. Schiller (Ed.), *Instinctive behavior.*
New York: International Universities Press.
(By permission.)

Lorenz, K. 1969. Innate bases of learning. In
K. Pribram (Ed.), *On the biology of learn-
ing.* New York: Harcourt, Brace and World.
(By permission.)

Luria, A. L. 1968. *The mind of a mnemonist.*
New York: Basic Books. (By permission.)

Luttges, M., Johnson, T., Buck, C., Holland, J.,
and McGaugh, J. L. 1966. An examination
of "transfer of learning" by nucleic acid.
*Science*, 151, 834–837.

Mackintosh, N. J. 1969. Comparative studies
of reversal and probability of learning:
Rats, birds, and fish. In R. M. Gilbert and
N. S. Sutherland (Eds.), *Animal discrimination learning.* London: Academic Press.

Maier, S. F., Seligman, M.E.P., and Solomon,
R. L. 1969. Pavlovian fear conditioning and
learned helplessness: Effects on escape and
avoidance behavior of (a) the CS-US contin-
gency and (b) the independence of the US
and voluntary responding. In B. Campbell
and R. M. Church (Eds.), *Punishment and
aversive behavior.* New York: Appleton-
Century-Crofts.

McConnell, J. V. 1962. Memory transfer
through cannibalism in planarians. *J. Neuro-
psych.*, 3, 42–48.

McConnell, J. V. 1966. Comparative physiology: Learning in invertebrates. *Ann. Rev.
Psychol.*, 28, 107–136.

McGaugh, J. L. 1966. Time-dependent processes in memory storage. *Science*, 153,
1351–1358.

McGaugh, J. L. 1967. Analyses of memory transfer and enhancement. *Proc. Amer. Phil. Soc.*,
111, 347–351.

McGaugh, J. L. 1968a. A multi-trace view of
memory storage. In D. Bovet, F. Bovet-
Nitti, and A. Oliverio (Eds.), *Recent advances
on learning and retention.* Rome: Accademia Nazionale dei Lincei.

McGaugh, J. L. Unpublished findings.

McGaugh, J. L., and Krivanek, J. 1970. Strychnine effects on discrimination learning in
mice: Effects of dose and time of administration. *Physiol. Behav.*, 5, 798–803.

McGaugh, J. L., and Landfield, P. W. 1970.
Delayed development of amnesia following
electroconvulsive shock. *Physiol. Behav.*,
5, 1109–1113.

McGaugh, J. L., and Petrinovich, L. F. 1965.
Effects of drugs on learning and memory.
*Intern. Rev. Neurobiol.*, 8, 139–191.

Mehler, J., and Carey, P. 1967. Role of surface
and base structure in perception of sentences.
*J. Verbal Learn. Verbal Behav.*, 6, 335–338.

Melton, A. W. 1963. Implication of short-term
memory for a general theory of memory.
*J. Verbal Learn. Verbal Behav.*, 2, 1–21.

Miles, R. 1959. Discrimination in the squirrel
monkey as a function of deprivation and
problem difficulty. *J. Exp. Psychol.*, 57,
15–19. (Copyright 1959 by the American
Psychological Association, reproduced by
permission.)

Miller, G. A. 1956. The magic number seven
plus or minus two: Some limits on our
capacity for processing information. *Psychol.
Rev.*, 63, 81–97.

Miller, G. A., Galanter, E. H., and Pribram,
K. H. 1960. *Plans and the structure of behavior.* New York: Holt.

Miller, N. E., and Banuazizi, A. 1968. Instrumental learning by curarized rats of a specific visceral response, intestinal or cardiac.
*J. Comp. Physiol. Psychol.*, 65, 1–7. (Copyright 1968 by the American Psychological
Association, reproduced by permission.)

Milner, B. 1964. Some effects of frontal lobectomy in man. In J. M. Warren and K. Akert
(Eds.), *The frontal granular cortex and behavior.* New York: McGraw-Hill.

Milner, B. 1966. Amnesia following operation
on the temporal lobes. In C.W.M. Whitty
and O. L. Zangwill (Eds.), *Amnesia.* London:
Butterworths. (By permission.)

Milner, B., and Taylor, L. B. 1969. Differential
specialization of man's cerebral hemispheres:

Evidence from temporal lobectomy and from commissure section. *Symposium on Cerebral Dominance*, 9th International Neurological Congress. New York, September 26.

Moltz, H., and Stettner, L. J. 1961. The influence of patterned light deprivation on the critical period for imprinting. *J. Comp. Physiol. Psychol.*, 54, 279–283.

Moon, L. E., and Harlow, H. F. 1955. Analysis of oddity learning by rhesus monkeys. *J. Comp. Physiol. Psychol.*, 48, 188–194.

Morgan, J.J.B., and Lovell, G. D. 1948. *The psychology of abnormal people.* New York: Longmans, Green.

Morrell, F. 1967. Electrical signs of sensory coding. In G. C. Quarton, T. Melnechuk, and F. O. Schmitt (Eds.), *The neurosciences.* New York: Rockefeller.

Mueller, G. E., and Pilzecker, A. 1900. Experimentalle Beitrage zur Lehre vom Gedachtnis. *Z. Psychol.*, Suppl. 1, 1–288.

Newell, A. 1968. On the analysis of human problem solving protocols. In J. C. Gardin and B. Jaulin (Eds.), *Calcal et formalisation dans les sciences de l'homme.* Paris: Centre National de la Recherche Scientifique. (By permission.)

Newell, A., and Simon, H. A. 1963. GPS, a program that simulates human thought. In E. A. Feigenbaum and J. Feldman (Eds.), *Computers and thought.* New York: McGraw-Hill.

Newman, J. R. 1956. Srinivasa Ramanujan. In J. R. Newman (Ed.), *The world of mathematics.* Vol. 1, Ch. 13, New York: Simon and Schuster.

Norman, D. A. 1969. *Memory and attention.* New York: Wiley.

Olds, J., and Milner, P. 1954. Positive reinforcement produced by electrical stimulation of septal area and other regions of rat brain. *J. Comp. Physiol. Psychol.*, 47, 419–427.

Oliverio, A., and Bovet, D. 1966. Effects of age on maze learning and avoidance conditioning of mice. *Life Sci.*, 5, 1317–1324.

Osgood, C. E. 1952. The nature and measurement of meaning. *Psychol. Bull.*, 49, 197–237.

Overton, D. A. 1964. State-dependent or "dissociated" learning produced with pentobarbital. *J. Comp. Physiol. Psychol.*, 57, 3–12.

Pavlov, I. P. 1927. *Conditoned reflexes.* London: Oxford University Press.

Pavlov, I. P. 1957. *Experimental psychology and other essays.* New York: Philosophical Library. (By permission.)

Peeke, H.V.S. 1969. Habituation of conspecific aggression in the three-spined stickleback *(Gasterosteus Aculeatus L.). Behaviour*, 35, 137–156. (By permission.)

Penfield, W. 1969. Consciousness, memory, and man's conditioned reflexes. In K. H. Pribram (Ed.), *On the biology of learning.* New York: Harcourt, Brace and World. (By permission.)

Penfield, W., and Perot, P., 1963. The brain's record of auditory and visual experience—a final summary and discussion. *Brain*, 86, 595–696. (By permission.)

Penfield, W., and Roberts, L. 1959. *Speech and brain-mechanisms.* Princeton: Princeton University Press. (By permission.)

Peterson, L. R., and Peterson, M. J. 1959. Short term retention of individual verbal items. *J. Exp. Psychol.*, 58, 193–198. (Copyright 1959 by the American Psychological Association, reproduced by permission.)

Peterson, N. 1960. Control of behavior by presentation of an imprinted stimulus. *Science*, 132, 1395–1396.

Premack, D. 1970. The education of Sarah. *Psychol. Today*, 4, 54–58.

Pribram, K. H. 1954. Toward a science of neuropsychology (method and data). In R. A. Patton (Ed.), *Current trends in psychology and the behavioral sciences.* Pittsburgh: University of Pittsburgh Press.

Pribram, K. H., Ahumada, A., Hartog, J., and Roos, L. 1964. A progress report on the neurological processes disturbed by frontal lesions in primates. In J. M. Warren and K. Akert (Eds.), *The frontal granular cortex and behavior.* New York: McGraw-Hill.

Prisko, L. H. 1963. Short-term memory in focal cerebral damage. (Doctoral thesis, McGill University) Montreal, Canada. (By permission.)

Reiff, R., and Scheerer, M. 1959. *Memory and hypnotic age regression.* New York: International Universities Press.

Rescorla, R. A., and LoLordo, V. M. 1965. Inhibition of avoidance behavior. *J. Comp. Physiol. Psychol.*, 59, 406–412.

Ridgway, S. H., Flanigan, N. J., and McCormick, J. G. 1966. Brain-spinal cord ratios in porpoises: Possible correlations with intelligence and ecology. *Psychon. Sci.*, 6, 491–492.

Riopelle, A. J., Alper, R. G., Strong, P. N., and

Ades, H. W. 1953. Multiple discrimination and patterned string performance of normal and temporal-lobectomized monkeys. *J. Comp. Physiol. Psychol., 46,* 145–149.

Ritchie, B. F., Aeschliman, B., and Pierce, P. 1950. Studies in spatial learning. VIII. Place performance and the acquisition of place disposition. *J. Comp. Physiol. Psychol., 43,* 73–85.

Romanes, G. J. 1895. *Animal intelligence.* New York: D. Appleton.

Russell, W. R., and Nathan, P. W. 1946. Traumatic amnesia. *Brain, 69,* 280–300.

Searle, L. V. 1949. The organization of hereditary maze-brightness and maze-dullness. *Genetic Psychol. Monogr., 39,* 279–325.

Shandro, N. E., and Schaeffer, B. 1969. Environment and strychnine: Effects on maze behavior. Paper presented at Western Psychol. Assn. Meeting, Vancouver, B. C.

Shashoua, V. 1968. RNA changes in goldfish brain during learning. *Nature, 217,* 238–240.

Singer, J. L. 1966. *Daydreaming.* New York: Random House

Skinner, B. F. 1938. *The behavior of organisms: An experimental analysis.* New York: Appleton-Century-Crofts. (Copyright 1938, 1966, reprinted by permission of the publisher.)

Skinner, B. F. 1950. Are theories of learning necessary? *Psychol. Rev., 57,* 193–216. (Copyright 1950 by the American Psychological Association, reproduced by permission.)

Skinner, B. F. 1957. *Verbal behavior.* New York: Appleton-Century-Crofts.

Sluckin, W. 1965. *Imprinting and early learning.* Chicago: Aldine.

Smith, S. M., Brown, H. O., Toman, J.E.P., and Goodman, L. S. 1947. The lack of cerebral effects of *d*-tubocurarine. *Anesthesiology, 8,* 1–14. (By permission.)

Spalding, D. A. 1873. Instinct, with original observations on young animals. *Macmillan's Mag., 27,* 282–293. Reprinted 1954 in *Brit. J. Animal Behav., 2,* 2–11.

Spence, K. W. 1938. Gradual versus sudden solution of discrimination problems by chimpanzees. *J. Comp. Psychol., 25,* 213–224.

Sperling, G. 1960. The information available in brief visual presentations. *Psychol. Monogr., 74*(11), 1–29. (Copyright 1960 by the American Psychological Association, reproduced by permission.)

Sperry, R. W. 1968. Psychobiology and vice versa. *Eng. Sci. Mag., 32,* 53–61. (By permission.)

Spuhler, J. N., and Lindzey, G. 1967. Racial differences in behavior. In J. Hirsch (Ed.), *Behavior genetic analysis.* New York: McGraw-Hill.

Terman, L. M. 1916. *The measurement of intelligence.* Boston: Houghton-Mifflin.

Terman, L. M. 1925. *Mental and physical traits of a thousand gifted children, genetic studies of genius.* I. Stanford: Stanford University Press.

Terman, L. M., and Merrill, M. A. 1937. *Measuring intelligence.* Boston: Houghton-Mifflin.

Terman, L. M., and Oden, M. H. 1947. *The gifted child grows up, genetic studies of genius.* IV. Stanford: Stanford University Press.

Terman, L. M., and Oden, M. H. 1959. *The gifted group at mid-life, genetic studies of genius.* V. Stanford: Stanford University Press.

Terman, L. M., and Merrill, M. A. 1960. *The Stanford-Binet intelligence scale.* Boston: Houghton-Mifflin.

Thompson, R. F. 1967. *Foundations of physiological psychology.* New York: Harper and Row. (By permission.)

Thompson, R. F. 1969. Neurophysiology and thought: The neural substrates of thinking. In J. F. Voss (Ed.), *Approaches to thought.* Columbus, Ohio: Charles E. Merrill.

Thompson, R. F., and Spencer, W. A. 1966. Habituation: A model phenomenon for the study of neuronal substrates of behavior. *Psychol. Rev., 173,* 16–43.

Thompson, R. F., Mayers, K. S., Robertson, R. T., and Patterson, C. J. 1970. Number coding in association cortex of the cat. *Science, 168,* 271–273. (Copyright 1970 by the American Association for the Advancement of Science, by permission.)

Thorndike, E. L. 1932. *The fundamentals of learning.* New York: Teachers College.

Thorpe, W. H. 1963. *Learning and instinct in animals.* London: Methuen.

Tinbergen, N. 1951. *The study of instinct.* Oxford: Clarendon Press.

Tobias, P. V. 1970. Brain-size, grey matter, and race—fact or fiction? *Amer. J. Physiol. Anthropol., 32,* 3–26. (By permission.)

Tolman, E. C. 1932. *Purposive behavior in animals and men.* New York: Appleton-Century-Crofts.

Tolman, E. C., and Honzik, C. M. 1930. Introduction and removal of reward and maze performance in rats. *Univ. Calif. Publ. in Psychol.*,4, 257–275. (Originally published by the University of California Press; reprinted by permission of the Regents of the University of California.)

Tolman, E. C., Ritchie, B. F., and Kalish, D. 1946. Studies in spatial learning. II. Place learning versus response learning. *J. Exp. Psychol.*, 36, 221–229.

Tryon, R. C. 1942. Individual differences. In F. A. Moss (Ed.), *Comparative psychology*. New York: Prentice-Hall. (By permission.)

Tuddenham, R. D. 1962. The nature and measurement of intelligence. In L. Postman (Ed.), *Psychology in the making*. New York: Knopf. (Copyright 1962, reproduced by permission of the publisher.)

Tulving, E. 1969. Retrograde amnesia in free recall. *Science*, 164, 88–90.

Turing, A. M. 1950. Computing machinery and intelligence. *Mind*, 59, 433–460.

Underwood, B. J. 1957. Interference and forgetting. *Psychol. Rev.*, 64, 49–60. (Copyright 1957 by the American Psychological Association, reproduced by permission.)

Ungar, G. 1970. Chemical transfer of learned information. In W. L. Byrne (Ed.), *Molecular approaches to learning and memory*. New York: Academic Press.

Van de Greer, J. P., and Jaspars, J.M.F. 1966. Cognitive functions. *Ann. Rev. Psychol.*, 17, 145–176.

Van Ormer, E. B. 1932. Retention after intervals of sleep and of waking. *Arch. Psychol.*, No. 137.

Von Frisch, K. 1953. *The dancing bees*. New York: Harcourt, Brace, (By permission of the publisher.)

Waisman, H. A., and Harlow, H. F. 1965. Experimental phenylketonuria in monkeys *Science*, 147, 685–695.

Warren, J. M. 1965. Primate learning in comparative perspective. In. A. M. Schrier, H. F. Harlow, and F. Stallnitz (Ed.), *Behavior of nonhuman primates*. Vol. 1. New York: Academic Press. (By permission.)

Washburn, S. L. 1963. The study of race, *Amer. Anthropol.*, 65, 521–531. (Reproduced by permission of the American Anthropological Association.)

Wechsler, D. 1958. *The measurement and appraisal of adult intelligence* (4th ed.). Baltimore: Williams and Wilkins.

Weinberger, N. M., and Lindsley, D. B. 1964. Behavioral and electroencephalic arousal to contrasting novel stimuli. *Science*, 144, 1355–1357.

Wenner, A. M. 1964. Sound communication in honey bees. *Scient. Amer.*, 210, 116–124.

White, W. A. 1926. *Outlines of psychiatry*. New York: Nervous and Mental Disease Publ. Co.

Whitty, C.W.M., and Zangwill, O. L. (Eds.). 1966. *Amnesia*. London: Butterworths.

Wicklegren, W. A. 1965. Acoustic similarity and retroactive interference in short term memory. *J. Verbal Learn. Verbal Behav.*, 4, 53–61.

Woolf, L. I., Griffiths, R., Montcrieff, A., Coates, S., and Dillistone, F. 1958. Dietary treatment of phenylketonuria. *Arch. Dis. Child.*, 33, 31.

Wyers, E. J., Peeke, H.V.S., Williston, J. S., and Herz, M. J. 1968. Retroactive impairment of passive avoidance learning by stimulation of the caudate nucleus. *Exp. Neurol.*, 22, 35–36.

Yerkes, R. M. (Ed.). 1921. Psychological examining in the U. S. Army. *Memoirs of the Nat. Acad. Sci.*, No. 15.

Zemp, J. W., Wilson, J. E., Schlesinger, K., Boggan, W. O., and Glassman, E. 1966. Brain function and macromolecules. I. Incorporation of uridine into mouse brain during short-term training experience. *Proc. Natl. Acad. Sci.*, 55, 1423–1431.

Zener, K. 1937. The significance of behavior accompanying conditioned salivary secretion for theories of the conditioned response. *Amer. J. Psychol.*, 50, 384–403. (By permission.)

Zornetzer, S., and McGaugh, J. L. 1970. Effects of frontal brain electroshock stimulation on EEG activity and memory in rats: Relationship to ECS-produced retrograde amnesia. *J. Neurobiol.*, 1, 379–394.

# INDEX

# BEHAVIORAL
# OBJECTIVES

## CHAPTER ONE:  LEARNING

The student should be able to:

1. *Discuss* learning as a type of biological adaptation.
2. *Distinguish* between habituation, adaptation, and fatigue.
3. *List* and *describe* the characteristics of classical conditioning.
4. *Design* an experimental situation which illustrates instrumental conditioning.
5. *Compare* the roles of reinforcement in learning and in performing learned responses.
6. *Discuss* the reasons for very cautious consideration of species differences in learning abilities.

The student should *memorize* the following definitions:

*Classical conditioning*    a form of learning or training based upon the association of an unconditioned stimulus (US), one which initially evokes some response, and a conditioned stimulus (CS), one which does not initially evoke a response; presentations of US and CS are in a fixed order and are not contingent upon the subject's behavior

*Conditioned response*    a response learned by classical conditioning; the response to the conditioned stimulus

*Conditioned stimulus*    a stimulus which does not initially evoke a response in a classical conditioning situation; a neutral stimulus; a stimulus which evokes a conditioned response

*Criterion*    a standard against which performance can be compared; the level of performance required for mastery or learning

*Critical period*    a period of time in development during which the potential for acquiring some trait is optimal

*Discrimination reversal*    learning to respond to a previously incorrect choice in a discrimination task

*Discrimination task*    a learning task which requires that a subject learn to discriminate or choose between two or more stimulus choices

*Extinction*    a decrease in the rate, number, strength, etc. of a learned response resulting from a lack of reinforcement

*Fixed interval*    a schedule of reinforcement in which the subject is given a reinforcement for the first response which occurs following a predetermined interval of time after the last response, the time interval being fixed

*Fixed ratio*    a schedule of reinforcement in which the subject is given one reinforcement for a fixed number of responses

*Habituation*    a specific decrease in response to a repeated stimulus; a simple form of learning

*Higher-order conditioning*    Classical conditioning using a previously conditioned stimulus in place of an unconditioned stimulus, i.e., pairing one conditioned stimulus, which through classical conditioning has come to evoke a conditioned response, with some other neutral stimulus

*Imprinting*    the development of a strong attachment for some stimulus, usually the mother, experienced at a critical period after birth or hatching

*Instrumental conditioning*  also called operant conditioning, a method of training in which responses are rewarded or punished following their occurrence, thus shaping the behavior of organisms to the requirements of their environments

*Latent learning*  learning without any apparent reward or reinforcement

*Learning*  a more or less permanent change in behavior as a result of experience, excluding changes due to injury, disease, fatigue, etc.

*Learning set*  learning to solve a particular class of problems rather than one specific problem within the class; learning to learn

*Observational learning*  learning by imitation; learning by observing another individual performing the correct response

*Overlearning*  continued practice of some learned response after the learning criterion has been met

*Pavlovian conditioning*  also called classical conditioning; a form of training developed by the Russian physiologist, I. P. Pavlov; see classical conditioning

*Reinforcement*  the pairing of conditioned and unconditioned stimuli in classical conditioning; presentation of a reward or punishment following some response as in operant or instrumental conditioning

*Relearning*  a procedure for measuring memory in which the effects of prior learning are assessed by measuring the improvement on relearning the same material, i.e., by determining how much of the original learning experience was saved; also called the savings method

*Retention test*  a test that measures how much of an original experience is remembered

*Savings method*  see relearning

*Schedule of reinforcement*  the pattern of reinforcement relative to the number of responses, trials, time, etc.

*Sensitization*  an increase in response to repeated stimulation; an increase in response to presentations of an unconditioned stimulus not contingent upon pairing of unconditioned and conditioned stimuli

*Skinner box*  the animal testing cage designed by B. F. Skinner which includes a bar which an animal learns to press for reinforcement

*Spontaneous recovery*  a spontaneous increase in a learned response following a rest interval after extinction; a spontaneous increase in response following habituation

*Stimulus generalization*  a conditioned or learned response to a stimulus similar but not identical to the conditioned stimulus which was used in original learning; responding to one stimulus as if it were another similar stimulus

*Unconditioned response*  a response evoked by an unconditioned stimulus; an unlearned response; a reflex

*Unconditioned stimulus*  a stimulus which initially evokes a response in a classical conditioning situation; generally, a stimulus which evokes an unlearned response

# CHAPTER TWO:  MEMORY

The student should be able to:

1. *Discuss* the way in which studies of retroactive interference suggest the existence of a short-term memory process.
2. *Design* an experiment which demonstrates a
   a. retrograde amnesia gradient
   b. retrograde facilitation gradient
3. *Describe* the consolidation hypothesis of memory.
4. *Describe* experiments which suggest an influence of sleep on memory processes.

5. *Distinguish* between recognition, recall and relearning.
6. *Compare* proactive interference and decay theories of forgetting.
7. *Describe* evidence supporting the position that RNA is involved in memory processing.


The student should *memorize* the following definitions:

*Amnesia*   a loss of memory, generally caused by accidental brain damage; a loss of memory caused by experimental means

*Anterograde amnesia*   amnesia for events following the precipitating cause of the amnesia such as brain damage, electroconvulsive shock, etc.

*Consolidation*   the time-dependent process by which memories become stable or are stored in memory

*Digit span*   the number of digits that can be remembered over a short period of time

*Eidetic imagery*   an image-like form of memory found in certain individuals, particularly children, in which images of detailed scenes can be remembered for many minutes and longer under appropriate conditions; often called photographic memory

*Electroconvulsive shock*   a treatment in which electrical current of sufficient strength and duration to produce convulsions is passed through the brain for a brief period of time

*Engram*   the individual unit of memory

*Iconic memory*   very short term memory in human subjects, as for objects displayed very briefly; often called attention span or span of apprehension

*Long-term memory*   the ability to remember an experience over extended periods of time, such as days or years

*Proactive interference*   the interfering effect on memory caused by experiences which occur prior to original learning and attempted recall

*Recall*   a procedure for measuring retention in which a subject is asked to produce originally learned material from memory

*Recognition*   the simplest procedure for measuring memory in which originally learned material is presented again and the subject is asked if he recognizes it

*Retroactive interference*   the interference with memory caused by experiences which occur during the interval between original learning and attempted recall

*Retrograde amnesia*   amnesia for events prior to the precipitating cause of the amnesia, such as accidental brain damage, electroconvulsive shock, etc.

*Short-term memory*   the ability to remember an experience for a few seconds or minutes

*Split brain*   the condition in which the two cerebral hemispheres are disconnected by cutting the interconnecting commissures, particularly the corpus callosum, allowing the hemispheres to function independently of each other


# CHAPTER THREE:   THOUGHT AND LANGUAGE


The student should be able to:

1. *Explain* why Descartes' ideas of the nature of mind are useless as a scientific theory.
2. *List* three types of nondirected thinking.
3. *Distinguish between* directed and non-directed thought.
4. *List* and *describe* several experimental demonstrations of directed thinking in non-human organisms.
5. *Describe* the different thought processes attributed to frontal and posterior association regions of the primate brain.

6. *Compare* language and communication.
7. *Describe* the essential features of the following theories of language acquisition:
   a. reinforcement theory
   b. mediation theory
   c. generative theory.
8. *Discuss* the biological evidence supporting the generative theory.


The student should *memorize* the following definitions:

*Aphasia*   an impairment of language behavior following brain damage

*Communication*   communicative type of interaction between individuals which lacks grammar or syntax such as bird calls, distress cries, etc.

*Concept*   a general category that includes several objects or terms within it, on the basis of which an individual can make nominal classificatory statements or responses about a particular stimulus or class or stimuli

*Consciousness*   a measure of the sum total that an individual can describe about his own experience at any given point in time; an organism's state of arousal

*Deductive logic*   the application of a general rule or concept to prove or disprove a particular hypothesis or example

*Delayed-reaction task*   a task which involves withholding a response to a stimulus for a specified period of time following the presentation of the stimulus; a task in which responding must be delayed

*Generative theory*   a theory of language development which holds that there is a universal, innate language structure or syntax, and that all specific languages are simply variations on this universal structure

*Grammar*   refers to all the rules for correct use of a language

*Hypothetical construct*   an inferred phenomenon or process: for example; learning, gravity, mind, and other nonobservable phenomena

*Indo-European languages*   the largest family of languages in the world, including most of the languages of the modern western world

*Inductive logic*   the establishment of a general rule or concept to cover many specific examples; the formation of concepts

*Insight learning*   the sudden development of a concept

*Language*   communication between individuals which possesses grammar and syntax

*Morpheme*   the smallest units of speech that have meaning

*Nondirected thought*   thinking such as daydreaming or fantasy which is not directed toward the solution of a particular problem or task

*Pheromone*   a specific chemical which is released by one organism as a signal to another member of the same species; a chemical communicator

*Phenome*   an elementary speech sound of which there are about 40 in modern English

*Preconscious*   knowledge of which an individual is unaware at any given point in time, without necessarily motivational qualities

*Psycholinguistics*   the study of how humans acquire and use language

*Semantic differential*   a method developed by Osgood for analyzing the meaning of words.

*Sino-Tibetan languages*   the second largest family of languages in the world

*Speech*   vocal communication

*Syntax*   refers to that part of grammar concerned with the ordering of words, as in a sentence

*Turing machine*   a computer designed to simulate human thought processes

*Unconscious*   the totality of past experience and current existence of an individual of which he is not conscious at any given point in time, particularly unconscious motivation

*Umweg problem*   a problem in which some goal object can be reached only indirectly, as for example going away from food behind a barrier in order to circumnavigate the obstruction to direct access

# CHAPTER FOUR: INTELLIGENCE

The student should be able to:

1. *Compare* intelligence with IQ. *Explain* why the terms should not be used interchangeably.
2. *Give* the formula for computing IQ.
3. *Discuss* the attempts to find the biological differences between more and less intelligent brains.
4. *Describe* the usefulness of twin studies examining the question of inheritance vs experience as determinants of I.Q. (Note that intelligence provides a very good example of nature-nurture interactions.)
5. *Explain* the rationale for believing that making comparisons of intelligence between different species on the basis of any one aptitude is not a good practice.


The student should *memorize* the following definitions:

*Heritability*   the proportion of phenotypic variability due to genetic differences among members of a population

*Idiot savant*   rare individual who, although possessing an extremely low I.Q., has some extraordinary memory ability such as the ability to calculate past and future calendar dates, etc.

*Intelligence*   usually defined as that which is measured by an intelligence test; synonymous with intelligent behavior, also used in certain instances to mean adaptive behavior, ability to think abstractly, ability to learn, etc.

*Kwashiorkor*   a disease commonly seen in the children of countries where diets are deficient in protein, often accompanied by longlasting deficits in mental functioning

*Mental age*   the age of an individual as judged by intelligence test scores of the individual compared to average scores of groups of individuals at various ages

*Phynylketonuria*   a disease characterized by mental retardation which results from a hereditary inability to metabolize dietary phenylalanine

# MULTIPLE CHOICE
# TEST

## CHAPTER ONE:  LEARNING

1. Which of the following represents a decrease in responsiveness to all stimulation within a given sensory modality:
   a. classical conditioning
   b. habituation
   c. sensitization
   d. sensory adaptation
   e. fatigue

2. Learning cannot occur in which of the following preparations:
   a. single-celled organisms
   b. insects
   c. spinal cord
   d. fish
   e. none of the above

3. In Pavlov's classic experiments, pairing a stimulus with meat powder was called:
   a. extinction
   b. generalization
   c. reinforcement
   d. variable ratio
   e. calcification

4. Pavlov used a bell as a signal for meat powder; the bell is called a(an):
   a. conditioned stimulus
   b. conditioned response
   c. unconditioned response
   d. unconditioned stimulus
   e. generalization gradient

5. In Groves' and Thompson's experiment on habituation in the spinal cord, which type of interneuron showed only a decrease in response to the repetitive stimulus (habituation):
   a. type S
   b. type H
   c. type N
   d. type R
   e. all of the above

6. Pairing one CS with another CS is the procedure used to obtain:
   a. extinction
   b. generalization
   c. higher order conditioning
   d. habituation
   e. spontaneous recovery

7. In a training session following experimental extinction, a phenomenon appears at the very beginning of the training session termed:
   a. subzero extinction
   b. higher order conditioning
   c. spontaneous recovery
   d. latent learning
   e. response threshold

8. Which of the following response parameters is the usually measured one in experiments involving operant conditioning:
   a. response strength
   b. response rate
   c. response speed
   d. response duration
   e. response height

9. It was believed for many years, but subsequently disproved, that the following types of responses could not be modified by operant conditioning:
   a. autonomic nervous system responses
   b. skeletal muscle response
   c. verbal responses
   d. somatic nervous system responses
   e. central nervous system responses

10. Which of the following types of responses have been modified successfully using operant conditioning with electrical stimulation of the brain as a reward:
    a. intestinal contractions
    b. heart rate
    c. pupillary dilation
    d. 1 and 2 above
    e. 2 and 3 above

NOTE:    Multiple Choice Answer Key on Page 150

11. Rats given food pellets of two different sizes, with either sugar coatings or flour coating, if shocked every time they eat one of a given size or flavor will learn to associate the shock with:
    a. flavor
    b. size
    c. flavor and size
    d. neither flavor nor size
    e. always flavor but sometimes size

12. The distinction between learning and performance has been most clearly emphasized in studies of:
    a. classical conditioning
    b. instrumental conditioning
    c. latent learning
    d. habituation
    e. verbal learning

13. Which of the following factors affects the learning of a response but not the performance of it:
    a. motivation
    b. previous learning
    c. age of the animal
    d. health of the animal
    e. none of the above

14. It is probably an accurate statement to say that learning most often involves the acquisition of:
    a. specific responses
    b. muscle movements
    c. new responses
    d. specific stimulus-response relationships
    e. none of the above

15. Latent learning can be distinguished from operant and classical conditioning because of the following:
    a. it involves punishment
    b. it involves nonbiological rewards
    c. it invariably uses hunger as a source of motivation
    d. it does not involve rewards or punishment
    e. it is extremely rapid

16. If a sheep is trained to lift its leg in response to a tone which signals impending shock, then the sheep is placed on its back with its head on the shock electrodes, what will it do when the bell comes on:
    a. lift its head
    b. flex its leg
    c. extend its leg
    d. flex all four legs
    e. extend all four legs

17. Which of the following is most clearly an example of imitational learning:
    a. latent learning
    b. learning of songs by songbirds
    c. learning to walk
    d. learning to ride a bicycle
    e. all of the above

18. What is the most critical (optimal) age of young ducklings in order for imprinting to occur:
    a. 5 minutes after hatching
    b. 1 week after hatching
    c. 16 hours after hatching
    d. 48 hours after hatching
    e. 3 weeks after hatching

19. Which of the following animals performs most effectively and learns most rapidly in a learning set training paradigm:
    a. cat
    b. rat
    c. squirrel monkey
    d. squirrels
    e. rhesus monkey

20. The most complex form of learning appears to be the acquisition of:
    a. conditioned responses
    b. language
    c. learning set
    d. discrimination learning
    e. inhibitory avoidance

## CHAPTER TWO: MEMORY

1. The case of H.M., in which he could acquire no new information in long term memory, involved bilateral surgical removal of:
    a. parietal lobes
    b. temporal lobes
    c. occipital lobes
    d. frontal lobes
    e. none of the above

2. Very short term memory seems to involve the use of:
    a. gradients
    b. pictures
    c. details
    d. images
    e. apprehension

3. It is known that short term memory can be affected by interfering material which is acoustically:
   a. familiar
   b. different
   c. common
   d. intense
   e. similar

4. Hebb showed that college students could memorize series of nine digits, especially those series which were:
   a. repeated every tenth trial
   b. randomized from trail to trial
   c. repeated every third trial
   d. unfamiliar
   e. unsequential

5. Short term retention of information can be affected by experiences occurring prior to original learning and retention test, a form of interference called:
   a. retroactive interference
   b. proactive interference
   c. negative interference
   d. retrograde interference
   e. retention interference

6. A useful method for producing retrograde amnesia in laboratory animals involves the administration of:
   a. chlorpromazine
   b. electroconvulsive shock
   c. strychnine
   d. metrazol
   e. hallucinogenic drugs

7. There is extensive evidence that retrograde amnesia can be produced by drugs that inhibit the synthesis of:
   a. glucose
   b. foodstuffs
   c. carbohydrates
   d. proteins
   e. lipids

8. A treatment reported to enhance memory storage in mice or rats is:
   a. picrotoxin injections
   b. reticular formation stimulation
   c. strychnine implant in the reticular formation
   d. pentylenetetraxol injection
   e. all of the above

9. The theory that memory storage involves time-dependent processes which can be disrupted at periods prior to the actual memory storage is called the:
   a. consolidation hypothesis
   b. proactive interference theory
   c. acuity hypothesis
   d. metriculation theory
   e. additive memory hypothesis

10. Much of the evidence on retrograde facilitation of memory suggests that treatment producing this type of memory enhancement act on:
    a. sleep processes
    b. forgetting
    c. arousal
    d. coordination
    e. visual acuity

11. Retention of newly learned material may be better if it is learned:
    a. during sleep
    b. upon waking
    c. just before sleep
    d. in the morning
    e. under sodium amytal

12. Which of the following techniques is probably the easiest way of obtaining evidence of memory:
    a. recall
    b. learning
    c. relearning
    d. retrieval
    e. recognition

13. In recalling some previously learned material, the following feature of words is most important:
    a. the second letter
    b. the first letter
    c. the middle letters
    d. the visual image
    e. none of the above

14. The influence of the internal and/or external environments on memory is termed:
    a. retrograde dependency
    b. facilitation
    c. savings
    d. state dependency
    e. environmental facilitation

15. Ebbinghaus and others have found that over a period of days or weeks the most forgetting occurs:
    a. within one week
    b. within the last 24 hours
    c. within the first 24 hours
    d. evenly over a period of weeks
    e. evenly over several days

16. In goldfish, decay or disintegration of long term memory over a period of retention of several weeks is known to be related to:
    a. the color of their water
    b. the size of their aquarium
    c. the size of the goldfish
    d. the temperature of the water
    e. the number of fish in a given tank

17. Retention of a Y-maze discrimination by rats at long retention intervals appears to be improved by administration of:
    a. curare
    b. chlorpromazine
    c. acetylcholinesterase
    d. an inhibitor of acetylcholinesterase
    e. a protein synthesis inhibitor

18. The neurobiological process(es) that underlies memory can be said to be:
    a. precisely anatomically located
    b. completely understood
    c. not precisely anatomically located
    d. electrically based
    e. chemically based

19. Goldfish with a small polystyrene float attached to their jaws must learn to swim correctly and this activity is correlated with the ratio of:
    a. DNA to RNA
    b. glycine to uridine
    c. uracil to cytocine
    d. glycine to cytocine
    e. uracil to glycine

20. Taken together, the evidence that transfer of specific memories occurs is:
    a. conclusive
    b. unclear
    c. entirely negative
    d. all positive
    e. reliable

# CHAPTER THREE: THOUGHT AND LANGUAGE

1. The classical distinction between the mind and the body was proposed originally in the 17th century by:
   a. Homer
   b. Descartes
   c. Leonardo DiVinci
   d. Socrates
   e. Berkeley

2. In physical science, one example of a "hypothetical construct" is:
   a. a sate
   b. an electron beam
   c. wave motion
   d. gravity
   e. all of the above

3. The most reliable way to measure ongoing conscious thought of another individual is by means of:
   a. the EEG
   b. recording vocal movements
   c. verbal reports
   d. semantic differential
   e. opinion poll

4. The sum total that you can describe about your own experience at any given point in time refers to:
   a. the mind
   b. consciousness
   c. the unconscious
   d. knowledge
   e. thought

5. A particularly important contribution of Sigmund Freud, who founded psychoanalysis, was his suggestion that the following in many instances were unconscious:
   a. reflexes
   b. motives
   c. movements
   d. knowledge
   e. memories

6. Which of the following characterizes "poorly controlled" daydreaming:
   a. distractability   d. scattered thought
   b. boredom           e. all of the above
   c. self-abasement

7. A term meaning "self centered" and which characterizes the thought processes of many schizophrenics is:
   a. neurotic
   b. psychotic
   c. auditory
   d. autistic
   e. coherent

8. If an organism "has a disposition on the basis of which he can make nominal classificatory statements or responses," he is said to have formed a(an):
   a. S-R connection
   b. category
   c. unweg
   d. concept
   e. hypothetical construct

9. Which of the following concepts would be the easiest to learn according to the early studies of Hull, Heidbreder, and others:
   a. color
   b. square
   c. number
   d. circle
   e. bird

10. In the formation of the "oddity" learning set, each problem in a series of problems presents the subject with:
    a. 3 new stimulus objects
    b. 1 new stimulus object
    c. no new stimulus objects
    d. 2 new stimulus objects
    e. none of the above

11. Of the three types of rules for concept formation studies by Bruner, et al., the rule requiring that 2 stimulus attributes be present is called a(an):
    a. disjunctive rule
    b. conjunctive rule
    c. simple rule
    d. relational rule
    e. hypothetical rule

12. It seems fairly clear from an evolutionary point of view that the following neural structure is essential to the development of higher mental processes:
    a. reticular formation
    b. cerebral cortex
    c. hypothalamus
    d. rhinencephalon
    e. basal ganglia

13. The kinds of thought processes best described as "thought in time," seem to be at least in part elaborated by:
    a. posterior association cortex
    b. visual cortex
    c. the hypothalamus
    d. posterior motor area
    e. frontal cortex

14. In man, damage to posterior regions of the nondominant hemisphere produces loss of awareness of:
    a. auditory discriminations
    b. visual-sensory orientation
    c. motor coordination
    d. delayed response ability
    e. personality deficiencies

15. The following represents an instance of interspecies communication:
    a. the dance of the honey bee
    b. odor release by the Bomby moth
    c. human language
    d. distress cries of the baboon
    e. all of the above

16. The approximately 40 elementary speech sounds in modern English, as well as the elementary speech sounds of the other languages, are called:
    a. pheromones
    b. phenomes
    c. pronouns
    d. pharoes
    e. dialects

17. The theory of word meaning derived by Charles Osgood in part from the reinforcement theory of Clark Hull is called:
    a. the mediation theory
    b. the generality theory
    c. the reinforcement theory
    d. the meditation theory
    e. the differential theory

18. Children learning such diverse languages as Japanese, English, and Russian, apparently at the same point in language development learn the same:
    a. vocabulary
    b. superficial structure
    c. deep structure
    d. superficial grammar
    e. speech sounds

19. Permanent aphasia results from damage to the following area of the cerebral cortex in the adult:
    a. frontal cortex
    b. posterior speech area
    c. anterior speech area
    d. superior speech area
    e. all of the above

20. If the posterior speech area is destroyed in a child, he will subsequently reveal a new speech area which develops in:
    a. the anterior speech area
    b. the dominant hemisphere
    c. the nondominant hemisphere
    d. the superior speech area
    e. the frontal cortex

# CHAPTER FOUR: INTELLIGENCE

1. The first systematic attempts to measure functioning were made by:
   a. Darwin
   b. Romanes
   c. Galton
   d. Binet
   e. Cattell

2. A test which gives consistent results over time is referred to as being:
   a. valid
   b. persistant
   c. functional
   d. reliable
   e. standardized

3. A test which actually measured something that it was not supposed to measure would be called:
   a. not reliable
   b. not valid
   c. not consistent
   d. not standardized
   e. not functional

4. The 1904 intelligence test, the direct ancestor of modern intelligence tests, was developed by:
   a. Galton and Binet
   b. Darwin and Galton
   c. Binet and Simon
   d. Galton and Simon
   e. Simon and Darwin

5. The Stanford-Binet intelligence test was developed by:
   a. Terman
   b. Von Frisch
   c. Helmholtz
   d. Muller
   e. Beethoven

6. The Stanford-Binet intelligence test yields a numerical value called the:
   a. chronological age
   b. mental age
   c. intelligence value
   d. intelligence quotient
   e. mental quotient

7. If an individual's mental age, determined from the Stanford-Binet test, is one half of his chronological age, then his I.Q. would be:
   a. 100
   b. 150
   c. 50
   d. 200
   e. 75

8. Another intelligence test designed to apply to adults as well as children is called the:
   a. Wechsler scale
   b. formula test
   c. adult intelligence quotient
   d. piano scale
   e. absolute intelligence test

9. Bees signal the direction of a food source to other bees by which of the following means:
   a. speed of the agitated bee dance
   b. direction of the round dance
   c. duration of the waggle dance
   d. direction of the waggle dance
   e. emission of sounds

10. What percentage of individuals have an I.Q. above 130 points:
    a. 2.5
    b. 10
    c. 25
    d. 50
    e. 75

11. The brain of humans constitutes what per-
    cent of total body weight:
    a. less than 1%
    b. just over 12%
    c. just over 2%
    d. about 5%
    e. just over 8%

12. Which of the following measures provides an
    accurate indicant of overall intelligence:
    a. brain weight
    b. brain volume
    c. brain to body-weight ratio
    d. brain density
    e. none of the above

13. The following disease affects intellectual
    functioning by damaging cells in the brain
    with excessive body temperature:
    a. phenylketonuria
    b. kwashiorkor
    c. encephalitis
    d. alcoholism
    e. schizophrenia

14. Harlow and his associates have shown that
    it is possible to produce the symptoms of
    phenylketonuria in:
    a. rats
    b. cats
    c. monkeys
    d. dogs
    e. fish

15. Within a normal population of individuals,
    which of the following is the closest estimate
    of the heritability of I.Q.:
    a. .25
    b. .75
    c. .01
    d. .10
    e. .50

16. Which of the following factors can clearly
    affect I.Q. scores:
    a. heredity
    b. types of question on the I.Q. test
    c. cultural background of an individual
    d. emotional state
    e. all of the above

17. An indicator of reasoning ability and judg-
    ment which is somewhat independent of any
    formal educational experience is termed
    by Cattell:
    a. fluid intelligence
    b. intelligence quotient
    c. crystallized intelligence
    d. dynamic intelligence
    e. none of the above

18. The studies of identical twins discussed in the
    text indicated that the correlation coefficients
    between the I.Q. scores of identical twins were
    within the following limits:
    a. −.05 and +.05
    b. +.75 and +.95
    c. 0.00 and +.50
    d. −1.00 and 0.00
    e. +.50 and +.75

19. The difference in I.Q. scores reported for
    many ethnic groups probably results from:
    a. racial differences
    b. environmental differences
    c. hereditary differences
    d. differences in physiology
    e. differences in brain size

20. The type of intelligence proposed by Cattell
    which is most influenced by experience
    is termed:
    a. fluid intelligence
    b. abstract intelligence
    c. environmental intelligence
    d. crystallized intelligence
    e. solid intelligence

# MULTIPLE CHOICE TEST ANSWER KEY

## CHAPTER ONE:    LEARNING

| | | | | | | | |
|---|---|---|---|---|---|---|---|
| 1. d | 2. e | 3. c | 4. a | 5. b | 6. c | 7. c | 8. b |
| 9. a | 10. d | 11. b | 12. c | 13. e | 14. e | 15. d | 16. a |
| 17. b | 18. c | 19. e | 20. b | | | | |

## CHAPTER TWO:    MEMORY

| | | | | | | | |
|---|---|---|---|---|---|---|---|
| 1. b | 2. d | 3. e | 4. c | 5. b | 6. b | 7. d | 8. e |
| 9. a | 10. c | 11. c | 12. e | 13. b | 14. d | 15. c | 16. d |
| 17. d | 18. c | 19. c | 20. b | | | | |

## CHAPTER THREE:    THOUGHT AND LANGUAGE

| | | | | | | | |
|---|---|---|---|---|---|---|---|
| 1. b | 2. d | 3. c | 4. b | 5. b | 6. e | 7. d | 8. d |
| 9. e | 10. a | 11. b | 12. b | 13. e | 14. b | 15. d | 16. b |
| 17. a | 18. c | 19. b | 20. c | | | | |

## CHAPTER FOUR:    INTELLIGENCE

| | | | | | | | |
|---|---|---|---|---|---|---|---|
| 1. c | 2. d | 3. b | 4. c | 5. a | 6. d | 7. c | 8. a |
| 9. d | 10. a | 11. c | 12. e | 13. c | 14. c | 15. b | 16. e |
| 17. c | 18. b | 19. b | 20. d | | | | |